THE
COLORADO
14ers

SECOND EDITION

**The Colorado
Mountain Club
Foundation**

The Colorado Mountain Club Press
Golden, Colorado

The Colorado 14ers: A CMC Pack Guide
© 2006 by The Colorado Mountain Club Foundation

All rights reserved. No part of this publication may be reproduced or transmitted in any form or by any means, electronic or mechanical, including photocopy, recording, or by any information storage and retrieval system without permission in writing from the publisher.

Published by The Colorado Mountain Club Press
  710 10th Street, Suite 200, Golden, CO 80401
  303-279-3080 1-800-633-4417
  email: cmcpress@cmc.org
  website: http://www.cmc.org

Alan Bernhard: design, composition and production
David Hite: photo editor
Alan Stark: publisher

Cover photo of Mount of the Holy Cross by Terry Root

DISTRIBUTED TO THE BOOK TRADE BY:
Mountaineers Books, 1001 SW Klickitat Way, Suite 201, Seattle, WA 98134, 800-553-4453, www.mountaineersbooks.org

We gratefully acknowledge the financial support of the people of Colorado through the Scientific and Cultural Facilities District of greater metropolitan Denver for our publishing activities.

Contacting the publisher: We would appreciate it if readers would alert us to any errors or outdated information by contacting us at the address above.

WARNING: Although there has been an effort to make the trail descriptions in this book as accurate as possible, some discrepancies may exist between the text and the trails in the field. Mountain climbing and hiking are high-risk activities. This guidebook is not a substitute for your experience and common sense. The users of this guidebook assume full responsibility for their own safety. Weather, terrain conditions and individual technical abilities must be considered before undertaking any of the climbs and hikes in this guide.

Second Edition
ISBN 978-0-9760525-3-1

SECOND PRINTING

Printed in Canada

Contents

THE FRONT RANGE

SANGRE DE CRISTO RANGE

MOSQUITO RANGE

SAWATCH RANGE

ELK RANGE

SAN JUAN RANGE

SIDEBARS

GLOSSARY

APPENDIX 1

APPENDIX 2

An Introduction to the Fourteeners

The Fourteeners stretch across Colorado from Longs Peak in the Front Range in sight of Wyoming; to Culebra Peak, just north of New Mexico; to the San Juan Range near the famous Four Corners area where Colorado, Arizona, New Mexico and Utah meet. Climbing the Fourteeners will take you to many parts of Colorado and introduce you to a variety of flora, fauna, and rock, and even a little history.

An arrowhead found on the boulder field below the summit of Longs Peak, and a man-made shelter discovered at the apex of Blanca yield evidence that Native Americans did climb Colorado's great mountains.

Members of several surveys, especially the Hayden and Wheeler surveys, climbed many of the Fourteeners. A survey team climbed and named Mount Harvard and Mount Yale in 1869, while Mount Massive and Mount Elbert were summited in 1874.

Trappers and miners also climbed some of the great mountains, and prospect holes were found near the summits of Handies Peak and Mount Bierstadt, while abandoned cabins and mines dot the flanks of Mount Democrat and Mount Lincoln. Early climbers discovered evidence that grizzly bears may have used the summits of several peaks as habitat. A she grizzly "came rushing past us," reported a climber nearing the summit of Uncompahgre Peak in 1874. Claw marks were also discovered on the rock near the summit of Mount Sneffels.

The first record of someone climbing all of the then-known Fourteeners in Colorado dates to 1923 when Carl Blaurock and William Ervin achieved this feat. In 1912, Blaurock was one of the charter members of the Colorado Mountain Club (CMC), whose history is intimately tied to the exploration, mapping and even naming of Colorado's mountains.

"How many Fourteeners are there?" is a question that has intrigued climbers since the early days of exploration. A guide published in 1925 lists 47. Included in this ranking are Stewart Peak in the San Juan Range and Grizzly Mountain in the Sawatch Range, which later were demoted to Thirteeners. Missouri Mountain and its neighbor, Huron Peak, were added to the list in the mid-1950s after new measurements were made by the United States Geological Survey (USGS). Mount of the Holy Cross appeared on the list, was taken off, and then reinstated. By 1972, 53 peaks were recognized as Fourteeners. Ellingwood Peak in the Sangre de Cristo Range was the last peak to be added to the list. Today, 54 mountains are recognized as Fourteeners, both by the USGS and by the CMC.

How to use the Pack Guide

The organization of the Pack Guide is straightforward. The peaks are grouped by ranges in which they are found, and listed from east to west across Colorado. Within each range the peaks are cited from north to south.

The information on maps at the top of each description includes the USGS 7.5 minute map(s) as well as the Trails Illustrated map that you will need to do the route. Always have a map or maps of the route. Maps are available through your local outdoor store, or from www.usgs.gov or www.ngmapstore.com for Trails Illustrated maps.

The climbers who have shared their knowledge of the Colorado Fourteeners and suggested ratings in the Pack Guide maintain that there really is no "easy" mountain. Slippery cliffs, falling rock, crumbling ledges, heaving talus slopes and abrupt changes in the weather can turn a pleasant hike into a difficult climb. Thus, none of the mountains is ranked as "easy" to climb. Our rankings are "Moderate," "More difficult," and "Very difficult," all relative terms depending on weather, the climber's physical condition, and the time of the year. We do make a point, however, of telling you if a mountain is more difficult and if the climb can be dangerous.

Elevation gains are self-explanatory. Where two peaks are traditionally climbed in one day, the elevation gain and round-trip distance are recorded for doing both mountains. The elevation gain depends on where you start or where you camp; they are estimates.

The round-trip distance and estimated round-trip time are just that, estimates. The nearest town is a recognizable town on a Colorado state road map.

Some descriptions start out with a comment. These comments typically note mountains that are done together, difficult routes that require traditional climbing gear, objective dangers, and mountains with roads to the top.

Getting there is a section that describes how to get to the trailhead, and often, where to park once you are there. Some of these routes require four-wheel drive (4WD) vehicles with good clearance. We are not kidding about 4WD roads. The locals are vastly entertained when they come upon a rental subcompact on its side. And if you rent a 4WD at Denver International Airport, be careful; driving these roads is a little more tricky than you might imagine.

The route: The climbing routes are for summer and early autumn trips. Winter conditions can alter not only the route, but also the entire climbing experience. Distances are round-trip distances except when noted otherwise.

Sidebars consist of occasional observations, thoughts or rants that may be of help with climbing the Fourteeners.

Climbing the Fourteeners

The route descriptions cannot be relied upon as a substitute for good judgment and careful preparation. The guide makes no provision for the many variables that affect a climb, such as weather, physical condition of the participants and the possibility that climbers will fail to locate the described landmarks.

Climbers should use this guide with discretion and awareness of the countless hazards and challenges that must be confronted on even the "easiest" climbs. High mountains are subject to abrupt and drastic weather changes. Afternoon lightning storms should always be expected when climbing the Fourteeners from April to September, and some peaks do seem to have more storms than others. These peaks are also identified in the text.

Due to the frequency of early afternoon storms, summer climbs should be planned so that the party is descending from the summit by noon.

Despite what anyone may tell you, breathing almost three miles above sea level or climbing several miles upward at a high altitude will not only take your breath away, it will tire you quickly. The more serious physical discomforts climbers may encounter are nausea, headache and, occasionally, heart palpitations. There is an inherent risk in climbing mountains. Each climber attempting a Fourteener should be aware of the risk.

High altitude almost always means low temperatures and strong winds. Therefore, frostbite and hypothermia are possible dangers. Climbers can become exhausted or lost, or they may find themselves facing cliffs requiring technical rock-climbing skills. The consequences of climbing beyond your ability not only expose you to injury, but also endanger those hiking with you or coming to your assistance if you cannot go on.

We climb to challenge the limits of our bodies and our wills, and to test our capacity for risks. Yet, to go unprepared—carry no maps or compass, take an inadequate amount of water, or eschew a pack with warm clothing and rain gear—is simply dumb. On a Fourteener, a cloudless, sunny day can rapidly change to a snowstorm or a whiteout. Drinking unpurified stream water can expose you to waterborne parasites and a lightning strike can ruin your day. Be careful up there.

Access to the Fourteeners

As of the editing of this book in May 2006, access to the following peaks is not available: Mount Lincoln, Mount Democrat, Mount Bross, and Wilson Peak. Access to Culebra Peak is limited and on a fee basis. In the case of Mount Shavano and Mount Lindsay, land exchanges are being arranged with private owners. Check with the Colorado Fourteeners Initiative (303-278-7525) for up-to-date information.

The 10 Essentials

A properly equipped hiker will more likely than not have a successful outing. Essential equipment includes: broken-in hiking boots over wool socks on your feet and an extra pair of socks, wool or polypro, in your pack; quick-drying pants or rain pants, not cotton jeans; a lightweight wool or polypro shirt, not cotton; a hooded waterproof jacket or parka; warm head covering and gloves; and plenty of water, plus at least one meal and additional snacks.

The CMC has adopted a list, compiled by the Mountaineers of Seattle, of the "10 Essentials" that hikers and mountain climbers should carry in their day packs or backpacks.

These essentials are:
1. Map
2. Compass
3. Flashlight or headlamp
4. Extra food
5. Sun protection-hat, sunglasses, sunscreen
6. Extra clothing
7. A small first aid kit
8. Pocket knife
9. Matches
10. Fire starter

If you think you cannot carry the extra weight, perhaps you should reconsider your decision to climb a Fourteener in the first place. Some of the peaks require the use of a helmet, a rope, and occasionally, an ice axe. Climbers attempting these mountains should be familiar with belay and self-arrest techniques. It is also imperative that you tell a family member or friend where you are going and when you expect to return. And don't forget to sign-in at the trailhead if a register is available.

The Colorado Mountain Club

The CMC began placing registers on the peaks of the Fourteeners in the 1910s and 1920s. Old registers, which are available to researchers, are archived at the American Mountaineering Center in Golden, Colorado. Registers from the early years of the twentieth-century show that the number of climbers scaling the Fourteeners remained fairly constant until the 1950s. Climbing increased in popularity in the 1960s and 1970s, and exploded in the 1980s and 1990s. On a popular mountain such as Longs Peak, a register with room for 500 names fills in a week.

Registers are rolled up and stored in PVC plastic canisters secured at the summit by a cable or rock. Sometimes it is difficult to find the small, inconspicuous grey tube. Once you locate the canister, sign your name with a ballpoint pen or with a pencil. Signatures made with other sorts of pens tend to bleed on the entire register and obliterate names.

CMC members have also produced a number of mountain guides to Colorado's Rockies. The most exhaustive guide is the tenth edition of the *Guide to the Colorado Mountains*. Several detailed and useful guides to the Fourteeners, compiled by intrepid mountaineers in and outside the CMC, can be ordered by your local bookstore. These books are invaluable resources, particularly Gerry Roach's book, when planning ascents of the most difficult peaks.

John L. Jerome Hart wrote the first history of the naming and early ascents of the Fourteeners in 1925. As climbing Fourteeners grew in popularity, Hart's guide was reprinted in 1931 and updated in 1972. A new guide, based on Hart's but containing specific routes, was prepared in 1967 by Ray Phillips, another active CMC member. This guide was revised in 1978 by Sally Richards as the editor, with Jim Gehres and Al Ossinger preparing many of the updates. Jim and Al, as well as Giles Toll, are responsible for the trail updates in the previous edition. This Pack Guide would not exist without their input or the photographs donated by CMC members.

The Colorado Mountain Club Foundation

The Colorado Mountain Club Foundation (CMCF) was created in 1973 and supports expeditions to such far-flung places as the Himalayas and China. Since 1981, the CMCF has given grants to students in college and graduate school doing research in history, geology, geography, biology, and other aspects of Colorado's mountains. The CMCF also provides loans to the Wilderness Land Trust to permit the purchase of land when it becomes available in areas where trail access is restricted. The CMCF publishes brochures to educate hikers on hypothermia, lightning and snow avalanche, and distributes these materials free of charge to hikers through the CMC, the Forest Service, the National Park Service and outdoor retailers.

The CMCF also maintains a list of those who have climbed all of the Fourteeners and registered their accomplishment. At the time of publication, the list contained 1,156 names.

Individuals active in CMCF volunteer their time. Contributions to CMCF are tax deductible. All royalties from this Pack Guide will benefit the work of CMCF.

Climbers interested in the work of the CMC or CMCF

may obtain further information by contacting the club and the foundation at the American Mountaineering Center, 710 10th Street, #200, Golden, CO 80401.

Climbers who have completed all 54 Fourteeners should notify the Colorado Mountain Club Foundation at the above address to register their accomplishment and be included in the annual listing. Remember, an unwritten rule of the CMC is that a valid climb of a Fourteener entails an elevation gain of at least 3,000 feet. As with many rules, there are exceptions and the 3,000-foot-gain per peak rule does not apply when you are climbing two adjacent mountains, or where the access trail begins at a higher elevation, such as Mount Bierstadt.

Colorado Fourteeners Initiative

An estimated 500,000 hikers climb the 54 Fourteeners annually, a 10 percent increase per year over the number of climbers in the 1990s. While some of the remote peaks remain pristine, this increase in visits has seriously impacted many peaks, especially those in the Front and Sawatch Ranges. The Colorado Fourteeners Initiative (CFI) was formed in 1994 to mitigate the impact hikers have on the routes and alpine basins of the Fourteeners, and to ensure the long-term sustainability of recreation on these peaks. The following is CFI's Leave No Trace program specifically developed for the Fourteeners.

"Leave No Trace" Hiking

The Fourteeners are a harsh yet fragile environment. Above timberline, plants grow at the outer edge of life on Earth. Even slight human disturbances can cause long-term damage. Impacted areas may take hundreds, if not thousands, of years to recover.

To minimize environmental impact, the hiker should remain on the trail, especially in those areas where trail modifications have been made to reduce human impact. Because of the increased popularity of climbing the Fourteeners, ascents on weekdays not only minimize human impact, but also offer solitude and diminish trail and campground congestion.

The Colorado Fourteeners Initiative has developed these Leave No Trace guidelines that are specific to hiking and climbing the Fourteeners.

When hiking on a trail:
- Stay on existing routes and never cut across switchbacks;
- Walk through muddy or snow-covered segments of the trail, not around them.

When the trail does not exist:
- Travel on durable surfaces such as rock, snow and ridges, and avoid gullies or steep and loose slopes since these are prone to erosion and alpine vegetation loss;
- Disperse over a wide area if traveling in a group, to minimize the impact of stepping on fragile tundra.

When camping in alpine basins:
- Use existing campsites;
- Do not camp above timberline.

Consult the CFI website at www.14ers.org for volunteer opportunities on CFI trail crews and for CFI and Forest Service route recommendations and trail changes.

Longs Peak

14,255 FEET

MAPS	Longs Peak 7.5 minute, Trails Illustrated–301 Longs Peak
RATING	Very difficult
ELEVATION GAIN	4,850 feet
ROUND-TRIP DISTANCE	16 miles
ROUND-TRIP TIME	12 to 15 hours
NEAREST TOWN	Estes Park

COMMENT: Plan on a very early start and a very long day.

GETTING THERE: Drive south from Estes Park 10 miles on Colorado 7, then 1 mile west to a "T" junction. The left fork leads to the Longs Peak Ranger Station and parking lot, which is often crowded. The right-fork leads to the Longs Peak Campground, where sites are available on a first-come basis. Additional camping is available at backcountry sites where permits are required. Contact Rocky Mountain National Park (970-586-1242) for information.

THE KEYHOLE ROUTE: The trailhead for Longs is next to the ranger station. Follow a good, moderately steep trail 6 miles west to the boulder field at about 12,800 feet.

Continue west for about 1 mile to the keyhole ridge at 13,100 feet. From here, the route is well marked with yellow and red bull's eyes (otherwise known as fried eggs). Follow the route onto the ledges along the west side of the peak, up the rock through to the ledge junction, or spur. Turn southwest through the "narrows" to the "home-stretch" of slab rock. Then continue to the large, flat summit. This is a long, tedious climb. There is exposure on the ledges, and the upper mountain can be dangerously slick with ice. Before starting, check with the Ranger regarding conditions. At certain times, an ice axe may be needed.

Longs Peak

© 2006 David Hite

Grays Peak
Torreys Peak

14,270 FEET

14,267 FEET

MAPS	Grays Peak 7.5 minute, Trails Illustrated 104–Idaho Springs
RATING	Moderate
ELEVATION GAIN	3,000 to 3,600 feet
ROUND-TRIP DISTANCE	8 to 9 miles
ROUND-TRIP TIME	6 to 8 hours
NEAREST TOWN	Silver Plume

COMMENT: These two peaks can be climbed in one day with a little more effort than it takes to climb only one. Weather, of course, can be a factor in deciding whether to attempt both peaks. Grays, the peak to the east (left), is usually climbed first. After summiting Grays, you then proceed to the saddle between Grays and Torreys, and climb Torreys. Climbers starting early can drive from Denver and return to the city that same evening.

GETTING THERE: From Denver, drive west on I-70 to Bakerville, Exit 221. Turn left over the interstate and drive south 3.5 miles on a steep, but wide and passable, dirt road to the vicinity of Stevens Mine at 11,300 feet. There is a parking lot for about 30 vehicles and outhouses are adjacent to the parking lot.

THE ROUTE: Take the iron bridge across the stream and follow a good trail that switchbacks for 3.5 miles. At about 13,500 feet, the trail forks. The climber has the choice of continuing up another 0.5 mile to the summit of Grays, or taking the trail west to the saddle between Grays and Torreys at 13,700 feet and climbing Torreys' ridge to the summit.

After climbing Grays, descend from the summit northwest 600 feet into the saddle on a marked trail and follow the ridge north for 0.5 mile to the summit of Torreys. The distance between the peaks is about 0.5 mile as the crow flies. There is usually an extensive snowfield at the saddle in the spring and early summer. Cross the saddle by post-holing. Try to remain on the trail to avoid trampling on the fragile vegetation on the edges of the snowfield. Proceed with caution.

From Torreys, return to the saddle, then work back to the trail down the north side of Grays. Early in the season, this route may entail a climb well up Grays' slope to avoid the usual snow cornice.

You may see mountain goats during the climb.

Because of the climb's popularity and to protect the tundra, the CFI has realigned part of the trail on the saddle. It is marked with cairns.

SIDEBAR: INTERSTATE 70.

We know. We know. I-5 on the west coast is probably one of the worse roads ever built, and virtually undriveable in a cold winter rainstorm. And I-95 on the east coast, "forget about it," as the locals say. If you can't get out there and play with the 18-wheelers, don't bother.

But we know of nothing quite like I-70 on a Friday or Sunday afternoon. Starting at about 2 P.M. on Friday, I-70 going west slows to a crawl, then becomes a parking lot that doesn't clear up until after dark. The same thing happens in reverse on Sunday afternoon.

To an out of town climber, I-70 looks like the best route to the mountains if you land at Denver International Airport. Don't do it if you can avoid it. Check out US 285 out of southwestern Denver and US 24 by way of I-25 south to Colorado Springs. Both are two lane highways, but tend to move relatively well.

Grays Peak

© 2006 Phil Schmuck

FRONT RANGE

Torreys Peak

© 2006 Phil Schmuck

Mount Evans

14,264 FEET

MAPS	Mount Evans 7.5 minute, Idaho Springs 7.5 minute, Trails Illustrated 104–Idaho Springs/Loveland Pass
RATING	Moderate
ELEVATION GAIN	3,000 feet
ROUND-TRIP DISTANCE	9 miles
ROUND-TRIP TIME	7 hours
NEAREST TOWN	Georgetown

COMMENT: Mount Evans has a paved toll road to the top that can be run or cycled, but watch out for the traffic. Since there is a paved road to the summit, there is no register. The climb can be done in a day trip from Denver.

GETTING THERE: Take I-70 west to Idaho Springs. Take exit 240 and follow the signs to Mount Evans Road.

THE ROUTE: Start from Summit Lake by hiking northwest around the lake to the start of the established trail up the ridge to Mount Spaulding. From Spaulding, follow the trail along the ridge to the summit of Mount Evans. Note: From Summit Lake, you will not gain the required 3,000 feet in altitude. The Colorado Fourteeners Initiative is building the route from Chicago Lakes basin to Summit Lake. That will provide hikers with a route that will give them the 3,000 feet of elevation gain.

You may see mountain goats during the climb, especially below Summit Lake or on the Sawtooth Ridge between Mount Evans and Mount Bierstadt.

SIDEBAR: RIDE A FOURTEENER.
The Bob Cook Memorial Mount Evans Hill Climb starts at 7,540 feet in front of the Clear Creek Middle School and climbs on the highest paved road in the United States to the Mount Evans summit, over a 28 mile route. The race phone number is 303-322-3420.

Mount Evans

© 2006 Phil Schmuck

Mount Bierstadt

14,060 FEET

MAPS	Mount Evans 7.5 minute, Trails Illustrated–104 Idaho Springs/ Loveland Pass
RATING	Moderate
ELEVATION GAIN	2,900 feet
ROUND-TRIP DISTANCE	6 miles
ROUND-TRIP TIME	6 to 8 hours
NEAREST TOWN	Georgetown

COMMENT: Both Mount Bierstadt and Mount Evans may be climbed in one day. However, the Sawtooth Ridge connecting the two mountains is exposed and is difficult if you are not a rock climber. Do not attempt this route unless you are confident of your abilities. Consult more detailed guides if you plan to do this traverse. Be especially watchful of the weather.

GETTING THERE: From Georgetown, drive south 11 miles along South Clear Creek Road to Guanella Pass at 11,699 feet. The peak is in view to the east-southeast.

THE ROUTE: Hike 1 mile on the boardwalk over the dreaded willows. The trail continues east, then south, to reach the west ridge of the peak. The trail then follows the ridge east to the summit.

SIDEBAR: THE DREADED WILLOWS.
Before the boardwalk was built the Bierstadt route worked its way through a willow swamp that was one of the worst approaches to any of the Fourteeners. There was no way to get through it with dry feet, and some idiot was always shouting, "Here's the way!" and he was always wrong.

Mount Bierstadt

© 2006 Phil Schmuck

Pikes Peak

14,110 FEET

MAPS	Pikes Peak 7.5 minute, Trails Illustrated 137–Pikes Peak/Canon City
RATING	Moderate but long
ELEVATION GAIN	7,400 feet
ROUND-TRIP DISTANCE	26 miles
ROUND-TRIP TIME	12 to 14 hours
NEAREST TOWN	Manitou Springs

COMMENT: This is a long hike. Before starting you may wish to inquire at the cog railroad about the possibility of taking the train down from the summit. Since there is a dirt road to the top of Pikes Peak, there is no register.

GETTING THERE: To reach the Barr Trail, drive to Manitou Springs and locate the City Hall. Proceed west on US 25 (business) about 0.5 mile to Ruxton Avenue. Turn left on Ruxton Avenue and drive 0.75 mile to the Pikes Peak Cog Railroad depot, then on for a short distance to the hydroelectric plant and Hydro Street. Look for the Barr Trail parking lot and park here, if there is room.

THE ROUTE: From the trailhead the route switchbacks and climbs steeply for 3.5 miles, then rises gradually for the next 2 miles. After passing the 5-mile mark you will see the Barr Camp. After the Barr Camp, the well-maintained trail climbs steeply to the summit.

ALTERNATE ROUTES: Drive up Pikes Peak Highway and park at 11,000 feet, then take odd trails near and along the highway to the summit. However, when tourist traffic is heavy, police may object to hikers being on this narrow road. You can also climb up the west side of the peak from the Crags campground near the town of Divide.

Pikes Peak

© 2006 Phil Schmuck

Kit Carson Peak

14,165 FEET

MAPS	Creston Peak 7.5 minute, Trails Illustrated 138–Sangre de Cristo Mountains
RATING	Very difficult
ELEVATION GAIN	3,500 feet
ROUND-TRIP DISTANCE	6 miles
ROUND-TRIP TIME	8 hours
NEAREST TOWN	Westcliffe

GETTING THERE: Approaching from the north, go 14 miles on Colorado 17 from the junction of Colorado 17 and US 285, or approaching from the south, go north 17 miles from Hooper on Colorado 17. From either direction, you next turn east on a paved road and travel 12.5 miles to Crestone. From Crestone, go east on Galena Street, reaching the trailhead after approximately 2 miles. From the Willow Creek trailhead, hike approximately 7.5 miles to the lake.

THE ROUTE: Take the trail around the north side of the lake and continue above the falls. It's a steep climb to Challenger Point. Over the point is the west side of Kit Carson with a shelf called "Kit Carson Avenue." The Avenue leads around the west face of the peak and goes up the south side of the peak.

SIDEBAR: 12,000 FOOT MANTRA.

After you pass 12,000 feet the going will get tougher. It helps to repeat three or four of these words, or words like them as a mountaineers mantra:

Words that will get you up the route if mumbled over and over again between breaths: relentless, implacable, resolute, stubborn, undaunted, intrepid, headstrong, stalwart, tenacious, persistent, tireless, enduring.

We have used *relentless–enduring–stubborn–tenacious* with some success.

Kit Carson Peak

© 2006 David Hite

Humboldt Peak

14,064 FEET

MAPS	Crestone Peak 7.5 minute, Trails Illustrated 138–Sangre de Cristo Mountains
RATING	Moderate
ELEVATION GAIN	2,400 feet
ROUND-TRIP DISTANCE	4 miles
ROUND-TRIP TIME	5 hours
NEAREST TOWN	Westcliffe

COMMENT: Of the four mountains in the "Crestones": Crestone Peak, Crestone Needle, Kit Carson, and Humboldt, Humboldt is the easiest.

GETTING THERE: From Westcliffe, drive southeast about 4.5 miles on Colorado 69 toward Walsenburg. Turn right (south) for 5.5 miles to the end of Colfax Lane, then turn right. You are now headed straight west toward the Crestones. After about 1 mile the road becomes very rugged, but 4WD vehicles with good ground clearance can be driven further, sometimes another 5 miles depending on conditions. From the turn-off from Colfax Lane, it is 7 miles to the South Colony Lakes at 11,700 feet. Camp near the end of the jeep road or at lower South Colony Lake, 1 mile up the trail.

THE ROUTE: From lower South Colony Lake, hike northwest on the trail up South Colony Creek to the east side of upper South Colony Lake. Follow the Humboldt Trail north up scree and talus to Humboldt's west ridge. Reach the ridge just east of the 12,850-foot connecting saddle between Humboldt and Crestone peaks. Climb east on the ridge for less than a mile to the summit.

Humboldt Peak

© 2006 Phil Schmuck

Crestone Peak

14,294 FEET

MAPS	Crestone Peak 7.5 minute, Trails Illustrated 138–Sangre de Cristo Mountains
RATING	Very difficult
ELEVATION GAIN	4,300 feet
ROUND-TRIP DISTANCE	6 miles
ROUND-TRIP TIME	9 to 11 hours
NEAREST TOWN	Westcliffe

COMMENT: A climbing helmet, rope, and ice axe are highly recommended for this route. There is residual ice on the couloir near the summit well into the summer, and an ice axe may be required. Falling rock presents another hazard, making the use of a helmet a very good idea.

GETTING THERE: From Westcliffe drive southeast about 4.5 miles on Colorado 69 toward Walsenburg. Turn right (south) for 5.5 miles to the end of Colfax Lane, then turn right. You are now headed straight west toward the Crestones. After about 1 mile the road becomes very rugged, but 4WD vehicles with good ground clearance can be driven further, sometimes another 5 miles depending on conditions. From the turn-off from Colfax Lane, it is 7 miles to the South Colony Lakes at 11,700 feet. Camp near the end of the jeep road or at lower South Colony Lake, 1 mile up the trail.

THE ROUTE: Follow the trail west past lower South Colony Lake, then past upper South Colony Lake to a high plateau at 13,000 feet called "Bear's Playground." The plateau is between the Crestones and Kit Carson. Head south up jumbled rocks to gain the steep, red couloir that culminates near the summit.

Crestone Peak

© 2006 Phil Schmuck

Crestone Needle

14,197 FEET

MAPS	Crestone Peak 7.5 minute, Trails Illustrated 138–Sangre de Cristo Mountains
RATING	Very difficult
ELEVATION GAIN	2,700 feet
ROUND-TRIP DISTANCE	3 miles
ROUND-TRIP TIME	6 hours
NEAREST TOWN	Westcliffe

COMMENT: This peak, once considered unclimbable, was the last of the Colorado Fourteeners to be summited. The various routes up the east face are technical climbs. Though it is a good climbing precaution to carry a rope, the west face, over sound rock, can, with care, be climbed unassisted. It goes without saying that a helmet should be worn on this route.

GETTING THERE: From Westcliffe, drive southeast about 4.5 miles on Colorado 69 toward Walsenburg. Turn right (south) for 5.5 miles to the end of Colfax Lane, then turn right. You are now headed straight west toward the Crestones. See Crestone Peak road description.

THE ROUTE: Circle lower South Colony Lake to the south and west. Climb southwest to the saddle between Crestone Needle and Broken Hand Peak. Continue northwest along the ridge towards the Needle. About 0.2 mile above the first bench, angle slightly right and look for a cairn-marked zigzag route on grass shelves. This route leads to the third pinnacle northeast of a low point on the ridge. Drop slightly into a narrow couloir and climb abruptly up to the summit. Look for a cairned route and follow it in your descent, otherwise you may find yourself on a cliff overhang and will have to climb back up or use a rope.

Crestone Needle

© 2006 Phil Schmuck

Mount Lindsey

14,042 FEET

MAPS	Mosca Pass 7.5 minute, Blanca Peak 7.5 minute, Trails Illustrated 138–Sangre de Cristo Mountains
RATING	More difficult
ELEVATION GAIN	3,600 feet
ROUND-TRIP DISTANCE	10 miles
ROUND-TRIP TIME	8 hours
NEAREST TOWN	Westcliffe

COMMENT: As of May 2006 access issues are being worked out. Contact 14ers.org for current information.

GETTING THERE: Two miles north of Walsenburgh, Colorado 69 intersects Interstate 25 at Exit 52. Take Colorado 69 for 25 miles to Gardner. Approximately 0.2 miles west of Gardner take the left fork onto an unmarked county road. Drive for 13 miles, passing the town of Redwing. Take the left fork onto Forest Service Road 407 in the San Isabel National Forest and continue 4 miles to a sign identifying the private property of Singing River Ranch. Park in an area downstream of the private property sign. Ranch owners do not permit parking or camping on their property. The next 7 miles to the road's end can be rough and are best suited for a 4WD vehicle.

THE ROUTE: From the end of the road, hike 1.5 miles on an old jeep road to the end of the marsh. Turn to the southeast and climb up the drainage to a large grassy basin southwest of the Iron Nipple. From the grassy basin, climb southeast to a ridge running southwest by northwest. Once on the ridge, climb northeast to reach the main northwest edge of Lindsey. Once on this ridge, climb souheast to the summit. Follow the top of the ridge from the saddle to the summit. At approximately 13,400 feet, a cleft in the ridge offers difficulty over one short, steep point. Beyond that point this route is not difficult.

SANGRE DE CRISTO RANGE

Mount Lindsey

© 2006 Phil Schmuck

Little Bear Peak

14,037 FEET

MAPS	Blanca Peak 7.5 minute, Twin Peaks 7.5 minute, Trails Illustrated 138–Sangre de Cristo Mountains
RATING	Very difficult
ELEVATION GAIN	2,300 feet
ROUND-TRIP DISTANCE	4 miles
ROUND-TRIP TIME	6.5 hours
NEAREST TOWN	Blanca

COMMENT: Steep slabs and falling rock make a helmet a "must have" on this route.

GETTING THERE: From US 160, 6 miles west of Blanca and 15 miles east of Alamosa, drive north on Colorado 150 for 3 miles to a rough road going east. Take this road that becomes progressively rougher and can damage a car. Drive as far as possible, then pack in to Lake Como at 11,700 feet. Camp at the east end of the lake or higher, near timberline.

THE ROUTE: Continue for 0.3 mile past the lake on the jeep road. In the flats southwest of Blue Lake, head southwest to an obvious couloir that leads to Little Bear's west ridge. Take the ridge until it becomes steep and jagged. Turn right (south) and contour for about 0.25 mile to a steep couloir that heads directly toward the summit.

SIDEBAR: REALLY STUPID?
There are few climbers who have summited every mountain that they have attempted. There are myriad reasons for not completing a route. There is no dishonor in a reasoned decision to turn around and go down. The mountain will always be there to attempt again. There is a simple question to ask yourself in deciding whether or not to stop and go down. The question is, "Is what I'm doing really stupid?"

Little Bear Peak

© 2006 Phil Schmuck

Blanca Peak

14,345 FEET

Ellingwood Peak

14,042 FEET

MAPS	Blanca Peak 7.5 minute, Twin Peaks 7.5 minute, Trails Illustrated 138–Sangre de Cristo Mountains
RATING	Moderate
ELEVATION GAIN	3,200 feet
ROUND-TRIP DISTANCE	8 miles
ROUND-TRIP TIME	8 hours
NEAREST TOWN	Blanca

COMMENT: Blanca and Ellingwood are traditionally done together. Done separately, the round-trip time for each mountain is 6 hours and the distance is 6 miles.

GETTING THERE: From US 160, 6 miles west of Blanca and 15 miles east of Alamosa, drive north on Colorado 150 for 3 miles to a rough road going east. Take this road that becomes progressively rougher and can damage a car. Drive as far as possible, then pack in to Lake Como at 11,700 feet. Camp at the east end of the lake or higher, near timberline.

THE ROUTE: Hike northeast up the basin, passing north of Crater Lake, to the Blanca-Ellingwood ridge. On the ridge, turn right (south) to ascend Blanca, or left to reach Ellingwood. Return to the saddle to descend.

SIDEBAR: CELL PHONES.

Take one with you. Turn it off. Cell phones don't work in the valleys and on approaches, but they sometimes work at altitude. There is always a fool on the summit attempting to talk to a significant other who could probably give a damn.

A cell phone is a radio. If there is an emergency, use your map or GPS (if you have one) to identify the location (longitude and latitude) of the incident and call 911. If your cell doesn't acquire a signal, keep going higher, and keep trying.

Blanca Peak

© 2006 Phil Schmuck

Ellingwood Peak

© 2006 Phil Schmuck

Culebra Peak

14,047 FEET

MAPS	Culebra Peak 7.5 minute, El Valle Creek 7.5 minute. There is no Trails Illustrated map for this peak.
RATING	More difficult
ELEVATION GAIN	3,000 feet
ROUND-TRIP DISTANCE	5 miles from high camp
ROUND-TRIP TIME	6 hours
NEAREST TOWN	San Luis

COMMENT: Access to Culebra is restricted. The owner allows 150 climbers per year at $100 each. Check with www.14ers.org for the latest information about access to the peak.

GETTING THERE: From San Luis drive south and southeast on Colorado 152 through the town of Chama. The road turns east and is paved for 4 miles beyond Chama, where it crosses two bridges that are a few hundred feet apart. Immediately past the second bridge, make a sharp right turn and follow the dirt road about 1 mile to where the road ends at a "T" junction. Turn left, then continue to bear right and drive 2 miles more. The ranch will be on your left. Follow directions given you as to where to park. In past years, parking was allowed beyond ranch headquarters.

THE ROUTE: After leaving the ranch keep right at the first junction, then take the center fork where the road branches at timberline. Follow this road to where it crosses the creek. Camp here. The distance from the ranch to the campsite is 4 miles.

From the camp, ascend the ridge at the low point to the east. Follow the ridge south, then southwest. Culebra's summit becomes visible at the highest point south of the ridge. Continue south, then southeast, on the ridge. There is a small loss in elevation and some rock scrambling near the summit.

Culebra Peak

© 2006 Benjamin F. Smith

Quandary Peak

14,265 FEET

MAPS	Breckenridge 7.5 minute, Trails Illustrated 109–Breckenridge/Tennessee Pass
RATING	Moderate
ELEVATION GAIN	3,300 feet
ROUND-TRIP DISTANCE	6 miles
ROUND-TRIP TIME	6 hours
NEAREST TOWN	Breckenridge

COMMENT: The route up and down Quandary is a favorite for backcountry skiers.

GETTING THERE: Drive west through the Eisenhower Tunnel on Interstate 70 and exit at Frisco, heading south on Colorado 9 toward Breckenridge. Continue south past the town for approximately 9 miles to where Colorado 9 starts to climb to Hoosier Pass. Make a right on Blue Lakes Road, marked as 850 (with a sign that looks like a street sign). You will be heading west up a canyon. Immediately thereafter, an unimproved road angles up to the right from County Road 850. Take McCullough Gulch Road (County Road 851) to a new trailhead and parking lot 0.1 mile from County Road 850.

THE ROUTE: The new trail is across the road, and leads west through timber. Near tree line, the trail swings to the south and follows the south side of the long east ridge of the peak. At about 12,900 feet, the trail joins the main ridge and continues over tundra and talus to the summit.

SIDEBAR: A DAY TO ACCLIMATE.

If you are coming from the flatlands to do a Fourteener, give yourself a break and spend 24 hours or so in a mountain town relaxing before you put-up a route. Go for a real easy run, drink a good deal of water and avoid alcohol.

Quandry Peak

© 2006 Phil Schmuck

Mount Lincoln   14,286 FEET
Mount Democrat   14,148 FEET
Mount Bross   14,172 FEET

MAPS	Alma 7.5 minute, Climax 7.5 minute, Trails Illustrated 109–Breckenridge/ Tennessee Pass
RATING	Moderate
ELEVATION GAIN	4,300 feet
ROUND-TRIP DISTANCE	11 miles
ROUND-TRIP TIME	8 hours
NEAREST TOWN	Fairplay

COMMENT: These routes have been closed by a private landowner due to liability concerns. Contact the Colorado Fourteeners Initiative (303-278-7525) for current information. Each mountain by itself is not difficult, but climbing all three makes for a long day.

GETTING THERE: Drive on US 285 to Fairplay, then north on Colorado 9 for 6 miles to Alma. In the center of town and across the street from a Texaco gas station, turn left (west) and drive 3 miles up Buckskin Creek Road (also called Secondary Forest Route 416) to 11,000 feet. Camp along Buckskin Creek Road if the climb is not a day trip from Denver.

THE ROUTE: Hike northwest up the road for 2.5 miles to Kite Lake, and from there follow the trail north 2 miles to the saddle. Climb Democrat 0.5 mile to the southwest. Return to the saddle and climb northeast for another 0.5 mile over Mount Cameron, and then an easy 0.5 mile to the summit of Mount Lincoln. Return to the Mount Cameron-Lincoln saddle and follow the gentle trail southeast 1 mile to Mount Bross. Return to Kite Lake for 1.5 miles down the west slope of Bross, taking the trail along the ridge. Continue down a couloir to the old road and back to the lake.

Mount Lincoln

© 2006 Phil Schmuck

Mount Democrat   © 2006 Phil Schmuck

Mount Bross

© 2006 Phil Schmuck

Mount Sherman

14,036 FEET

MAPS	Mount Sherman 7.5 minute, Trails Illustrated 110–Leadville/Fairplay
RATING	Moderate
ELEVATION GAIN	2,800 feet
ROUND-TRIP DISTANCE	9 miles
ROUND-TRIP TIME	8 hours
NEAREST TOWN	Fairplay

COMMENT: You can climb Mount Sheridan (13,768) first for a more interesting trip, then drop to the saddle and continue up the long ridge to the summit of Mount Sherman.

GETTING THERE: Drive on US 285 to Fairplay, then continue south past the town for about 1 mile. Turn west (right) on Park County Road 18 to Four Mile Creek. Drive 12 miles to the site of Leavick, a ghost town. Park here and find a campsite in the environs if you plan to camp.

THE ROUTE: Begin hiking on the road and pass the first mine, the Dauntless. The Day Mine Company of Leadville, which permits climbers to go through its property to the summit, owns the entire mountain.

Hike northwest up the most obvious road to the abandoned Hilltop Mine, then follow a trail up to the saddle between Mount Sheridan and Mount Sherman. Turn north (right) and hike up the ridge about 1 mile to the summit of Mount Sherman.

SIDEBAR: TRAIL RIGHT-OF-WAY.

The person coming downhill has the right-of-way because it is often easier to stop and step aside when you are going uphill than it is when you are going downhill.

Mount Sherman

© 2006 Deborah Atkinson

Mount of the Holy Cross

14,005 FEET

MAPS	Holy Cross 7.5 minute, Minturn 7.5 minute, Trails Illustrated–Holy Cross/Ruedi Reservoir
RATING	Moderate, but long
ELEVATION GAIN	5,400 feet including 960 feet on the return leg
ROUND-TRIP DISTANCE	14 miles
ROUND-TRIP TIME	12 hours
NEAREST TOWN	Minturn

COMMENT: When you review this route on your map, note that this is one of those routes, like the Barr Trail on Pikes Peak, where you lose altitude on the approach—in this case, almost 1,000 feet—that you gain and then lose and then have to gain again. On the way back down to your car you have to climb back up Half Moon Pass. It can make you a tad bit grumpy.

GETTING THERE: From Minturn, drive south on US 24 for 3 miles, then turn right (southwest) and drive on Forest Service Road 701 for 8.5 miles, passing Tigiwon Campground, to Half Moon Campground at 10,300 feet. Camp in this area.

THE ROUTE: Hike west 2 miles to Half Moon Pass at 11,600 feet. Descend 1.7 miles and 960 feet to East Cross Creek. Follow the trail west around a small lake 0.5 mile to the ridge and bear south up the ridge for 3 miles to the summit. Be careful on the descent not to drop left (west) into the West Cross Creek drainage. Remain on the north ridge of the mountain until the trail used during the ascent can be clearly identified descending into the trees at timberline.

Mount of the Holy Cross

© 2006 Phil Schmuck

Mount Massive

14,421 FEET

MAPS	Mount Massive 7.5 minute, Trails Illustrated 127–Aspen/Independence Pass
RATING	Moderate
ELEVATION GAIN	4,400 feet
ROUND-TRIP DISTANCE	13.5 miles
ROUND-TRIP TIME	10 hours
NEAREST TOWN	Leadville

GETTING THERE: From Malta Junction, which is about 3 miles southwest of Leadville on US 24, drive west on County Road 300 for 1 mile, then head south on Forest Road 110 for 5.5 miles to Halfmoon Campground at 10,000 feet. Camp or proceed another 1.5 miles west and park at the Mount Massive parking lot, where the Colorado Trail crosses the road. You can also park at the Mount Massive overflow lot on the left.

THE ROUTE: Take the Colorado Trail north 3 miles to the Mount Massive trail. Follow this trail through timber, then into a bowl and on to the northeast shoulder of the summit. This trail takes you very close to the summit, but some boulder scrambling is required near the top.

SIDEBAR: BOOTS.

It goes without saying that the boots you use on a Fourteener should be broken in. We have used everything from heavy, leather, steel-shanked mountaineering boots to trail running shoes. The old waffle stompers were just too heavy. The trail running shoes were ultra-light, but offered no protection at all. We have compromised with a high-topped, lightweight hiking boot made out of few discernable natural materials. These boots are light, tough, and they offer some protection, decent support and have an aggressive tread pattern.

Mount Massive

© 2006 Phil Schmuck

Mount Elbert

14,433 FEET

MAPS	Mount Elbert 7.5 minute, Trails Illustrated 127–Aspen/Independence Pass
RATING	Moderate
ELEVATION GAIN	4,400 feet
ROUND-TRIP DISTANCE	10 miles
ROUND-TRIP TIME	9 hours
NEAREST TOWN	Leadville

COMMENT: Mount Elbert is not a particularly striking mountain and the route is a walk-up, but Elbert is the highest Fourteener.

GETTING THERE: From Malta Junction, which is about 3 miles southwest of Leadville on US 24, drive west on County Road 300 for 1 mile, then head south on Forest Road 110 for 5.5 miles to Halfmoon Campground at 10,000 feet. Camp or proceed another 1.5 miles west and park where the Colorado Trail crosses the road. There is a large parking lot on the left and a sign that says, "Mt. Elbert Trailhead." There are also outhouses.

THE ROUTE: Hike south on the Colorado Trail for 2 miles to a well-defined fork in the trail. Turn right (west) at the fork and climb 3 miles up a rather steep trail (southwest) to the summit.

ALTERNATE ROUTE: From Colorado 82, take Lake County Road 24. Pass Lakeview and continue for 0.3 mile more. Take an unmarked road straight ahead where Road 24 turns right. Continue on for about 2 miles and park. Hike west on a rough road, which becomes a trail. The trail connects with the Colorado Trail. Watch for a sign for the Mount Elbert Trail that will take you to the summit.

Mount Elbert

© 2006 Phil Schmuck

La Plata Peak

14,336 FEET

MAPS	Winfield 7.5 minute, Mount Elbert 7.5 minute, Trails Illustrated 127– Aspen/Independence Pass
RATING	More difficult
ELEVATION GAIN	3,600 feet
ROUND-TRIP DISTANCE	10 miles
ROUND-TRIP TIME	9 hours
NEAREST TOWN	Leadville

GETTING THERE: From Leadville, drive toward Independence Pass on US 24, then turn west (right) onto Colorado 82. Continue for 14.5 miles. Look for a parking area on your left near the South Fork Lake Creek Road.

THE ROUTE: Hike along South Fork Lake Creek Road, crossing Lake Creek on a bridge and follow signs to the trailhead. The first mile of the climb passes through private property. Continue through forest and meadow to the ridge at 12,700 feet. Ascend the northwest ridge over talus and across steep rocky slopes. The cairn-marked route will take you to the summit.

SIDEBAR: WHEN YOU ARE FEELING PUKEY.

Acute Mountain Sickness (AMS) can strike just about anyone at anytime, at altitude. We've had flatlander friends get sick on the ride up I-70 at 8,000 feet and we've all, at one time or another, gotten AMS at different altitudes. It is simply hard to predict who will get it, or when. Apparently getting AMS is related to your physiology; some people can go from sea level to 14,000 feet with no ill effects at all, and some highly trained individuals get sick at 10,000 feet.

The symptoms of AMS are headache, nausea, loss of appetite, fatigue, dizziness and sometimes vomiting.

La Plata Peak

© 2006 Phil Schmuck

Mount Belford
Mount Oxford

14,197 FEET

14,153 FEET

MAPS	Mount Harvard 7.5 minute, Trails Illustrated 129–Buena Vista/Collegiate Peaks
RATING	Moderate
ELEVATION GAIN	4,600 feet to 5,900 feet
ROUND-TRIP DISTANCE	9 to 11 miles
ROUND-TRIP TIME	9 to 11 hours
NEAREST TOWN	Buena Vista

COMMENT: These two peaks are traditionally climbed together. The route between Belford and Oxford entails high altitude and exposure to whatever storms are lurking as you hike about a mile in each direction. Check the weather before proceeding since there is no shelter from sudden storms. These two peaks have a well-deserved reputation for sudden, violent, electric storms. Climb them early in the morning.

GETTING THERE: Drive north on US 24 for 15 miles, turn left (west) at Clear Creek Reservoir, then proceed 8 miles to Vicksburg at 9,700 feet. Small and primitive camp areas are along Clear Creek, east and west of Vicksburg.

THE ROUTE: Cross Clear Creek on a bridge at Vicksburg and hike south on a trail up Missouri Gulch for 2 miles, then continue along the creek until you reach timberline. You will see the route up Belford's northwest shoulder. Continue on the Missouri Gulch trail to the trail junction at 11,650 feet. The route climbs to the summit along a well-constructed trail. From the summit of Belford, find the trail that descends into the saddle between Belford and Oxford, dropping 700 feet. Watch the weather. Turn around if it looks at all bad. Continue east-northeast to Oxford. To descend, return to the saddle between Oxford and Belford. Return to Belford's summit via the same route. Descend using the ascent route.

Mount Belford

© 2006 Phil Schmuck

Mount Oxford

© 2006 Phil Schmuck

Missouri Mountain

14,067 FEET

MAPS	Winfield 7.5 minute, Trails Illustrated 129–Buena Vista/Collegiate Peaks
RATING	More difficult
ELEVATION GAIN	4,500 feet
ROUND-TRIP DISTANCE	9 miles
ROUND-TRIP TIME	8 hours
NEAREST TOWN	Buena Vista

GETTING THERE: From Buena Vista drive north on US 24 for 15 miles, turn left (west) at Clear Creek Reservoir, then proceed 8 miles to Vicksburg at 9,700 feet. Small and primitive camp areas are along Clear Creek, east and west of Vicksburg.

THE ROUTE: Cross Clear Creek on the bridge at Vicksburg and hike south on the trail up Missouri Gulch for 3 miles to the head of the gulch. Take the trail northwest up the tundra slopes and across a talus field to a saddle on the ridge. Do not head toward the rocks in the vicinity of Elkhead Pass since this is a dangerous way to the summit. Once on the ridge, proceed south-southeast along the narrow ridge trail to the summit. There is some exposure along the ridge trail.

SIDEBAR: SUMMIT TIME.

Don't be surprised on reaching the summit to find fifty or so other climbers sprawled all over the rocks.

The very first thing you should do when you summit is look around 360 degrees for a thunderstorm. Next check that everyone in your crowd is feeling okay, then sit down for a snack and rehydration.

We have spent as little as the time it takes to sign the register and beat feet downhill in front of a thunderstorm, and we have also lollygagged for an hour or so at fourteen thousand feet.

Missouri Mountain

© 2006 Phil Schmuck

Huron Peak

14,003 FEET

MAPS	Winfield 7.5 minute, Trails Illustrated 129-Buena Vista/Collegiate Peaks
RATING	More difficult
ELEVATION GAIN	3,200 feet
ROUND-TRIP DISTANCE	8.5 miles
ROUND-TRIP TIME	6.5 hours
NEAREST TOWN	Leadville

GETTING THERE: Drive south 19 miles from Leadville. Turn west on a gravel road running along the north side of Clear Creek Reservoir. Go about 12 miles, driving through the ghost towns of Vicksburg and Winfield. Drive just over 2.5 miles past Winfield on the rough South Fork Clear Creek Road to an old mine and parking lot. Leave your vehicle there.

THE ROUTE: The Huron Peak Trail is on the left of the parking lot. Follow the trail to a small creek, then cross the creek and continue up numerous switchbacks to the timberline at about 11,800 feet. Stay on the trail through a large grassy basin and gain the saddle between Huron and Browns Peak, which can be seen to the north. Ascend Huron's northern rocky ridge. The Colorado Fourteeners Initiative has done significant maintenance on Huron to reclaim the heavily eroded slopes. Stay on the ridge and follow the well-marked and cairned route to the summit. Avoid the large scree and talus bowl. Remain on the ridge for the descent and follow Huron Peak trail back to your vehicle.

SIDEBAR: THAT GURGLING SOUND.

If when breathing heavily at altitude you hear a gurgling sound in your lungs ... STOP and immediately go downhill; you have symptoms of High Altitude Pulmonary Edema (HAPE). Other symptoms are shallow breathing, fatigue and breathlessness while resting.

Huron Peak

© 2006 Phil Schmuck

Mount Harvard   14,420 FEET
Mount Columbia   14,073 FEET

MAPS	Mount Harvard 7.5 minute, Trails Illustrated 129–Buena Vista/ Collegiate Peaks
RATING	More difficult
ELEVATION GAIN	6,500 feet, both peaks
ROUND-TRIP DISTANCE	14 miles
ROUND-TRIP TIME	12 hours
NEAREST TOWN	Buena Vista

COMMENT: It is traditional to do both Harvard and Columbia on the same day if weather permits.

GETTING THERE: From Buena Vista, turn west on Chaffee County Road 350 (Crossman Avenue) for 2 miles, then north for 1 mile. At the sign, "North Cottonwood Creek," turn south for 0.2 mile, then west and northwest for 5 miles to the end of a passable road. Park here and backpack in.

THE ROUTE: After leaving the parking area, the trail crosses a bridge to the south side of the creek and proceeds westward 1.5 miles, to a trail junction just after the trail returns to the north side of the creek on a second bridge. Take the right-hand trail marked, "Horn Fork Basin," northwest, then west 2.5 miles to timberline. Camp in this area.

From camp, follow the North Cottonwood Trail 1.25 miles to the basin below Mount Harvard. The trail veers right, up and across a talus field near Bear Lake. Continue north up the steep grass and rock ridge. Proceed under the crest of the south shoulder of the summit block, and scramble up large boulders to the summit.

To traverse to Columbia, follow the east ridge of Harvard to the saddle at 13,440 feet. Next, drop off the ridge to the east and descend to the creek at 12,200 feet. Head south and a little west up grassy slopes, then over rocks to the summit of Columbia.

Mount Harvard

© 2006 Robert E. Thompson

Mount Columbia

© 2006 Phil Schmuck

Mount Yale

14,196 FEET

MAPS	Mount Yale 7.5 minute, Trails Illustrated 129–Buena Vista/Collegiate Peaks
RATING	More difficult
ELEVATION GAIN	4,400 feet
ROUND-TRIP DISTANCE	8 miles
ROUND-TRIP TIME	8 hours
NEAREST TOWN	Buena Vista

GETTING THERE: From Buena Vista, drive west on Chaffee Country Road 306 along Middle Cottonwood Creek for 12 miles. Park near Denny Creek trailhead and sign the register (right side of the road).

THE ROUTE: You will be following a wide trail and will make two creek crossings. When you reach a fork, bear right and proceed northwest for 0.25 mile to an intersection that should be marked. Take the right fork into Delany Gulch. Follow the trail to the south ridge and continue along the ridge to the summit. Descend the way you came.

SIDEBAR: A LIGHTNING PROTOCOL.

So you are caught in the middle of a thunderstorm and lightning is striking all around you, even below. You are remembering that the temperature of lightning is somewhat in excess of the temperature of the surface of the sun, that a fairly common lightning bolt can be 500 million volts, and that lightning often travels across wet ground.

What to do? Get off the ridge. FAST. Get off the trail because there's a good chance that it's a gully that can conduct lightning. Stay away from rock overhangs. Put your pack and rope on the ground as an insulator. Sit on top of your pack with your arms around your knees and your feet together, close your eyes, put your hands over your ears and think good thoughts. Try to be invisible.

Mount Yale

© 2006 Phil Schmuck

Mount Princeton

14,197 FEET

MAPS	Mount Antero 7.5 minute, Trails Illustrated 130–Salida/St. Elmo/Mount Shavano
RATING	Moderate
ELEVATION GAIN	3,200 feet
ROUND-TRIP DISTANCE	6 miles
ROUND-TRIP TIME	7 hours
NEAREST TOWN	Buena Vista

GETTING THERE: From Buena Vista, drive south on US 285 for 8 miles, then turn west on County Road 162 to Chalk Creek Road. Turn right at Mount Princeton Hot Springs Inn. Continue up along the road through the Young Life Camp and follow the road as far as the TV relay station at 10,800 feet. How passable this road is depends on the vehicle and the season. There is a good campsite where the stream branches.

THE ROUTE: Hike along the road for about 1 to 1.5 miles beyond the TV relay station to where the road emerges from timber, just short of the boulder field. From this point, the A-frame Young Life chalet is visible. About 100 yards farther, a trail leaves the road uphill to the right. The trailhead is not obvious unless you go too far and look back. Follow this good trail until within 0.2 mile or less of the mine at its end. Cut left, up a ridge that offers good access to the summit along a rocky, but usually dry, route.

SIDEBAR: GEARING-UP IN THE DARK.

On one very long route we saw a grad-student-looking fellow wearing two different shoes: a sloppy old leather shoe and a tennis shoe. When we asked him about the unique gear, he said he had camped the night before and put his shoes on in the dark and had not discovered his mistake until he was a mile or so from camp.

Mount Princeton

© 2006 Phil Schmuck

Mount Antero

14,269 FEET

MAPS	Mount Antero 7.5 minute, St. Elmo 7.5 minute, Trails Illustrated 130–Salida/St. Elmo/Mount Shavano
RATING	Moderate
ELEVATION GAIN	3,300 feet
ROUND-TRIP DISTANCE	7 miles
ROUND-TRIP TIME	8 hours
NEAREST TOWN	Buena Vista

COMMENT: Quartz, aquamarine and topaz crystals are common in this area and you may come across geologists and miners who have driven up to near the summit on the jeep road. This is not exactly your, "one with the mountain" climbing experience. It is more of a "four-wheel-drives-careening-downhill-get-the-right-of-way," sort of experience.

GETTING THERE: From Buena Vista drive south on US 285 for 8 miles, then turn west on County Road 162 for 9.5 miles to Cascade Campground. Camp here, and in the morning, drive another 2 miles west on County Road 162 to Baldwin Gulch Road at 9,239 feet. Turn left (south) and follow rugged Baldwin Gulch Road for 3 miles to a creek crossing at about 11,000 feet and park. This road is for four-wheel drives.

THE ROUTE: Cross the creek and follow the road until it begins to switchback up the broad slopes above you. Follow a convenient gully to by-pass the road and gain the south ridge of the peak. You may also stay on the road to just short of the summit. The final ascent is up a trail through talus.

Mount Antero
© 2006 Benjamin F. Smith

Mount Shavano
Tabeguache Mountain

14,229 FEET

14,155 FEET

MAPS	St. Elmo 7,5 minute, Mount Antero 7.5 minute, Garfield 7.5 minute, Maysville 7.5 minute, Trails Illustrated 130–Salida/St. Elmo/Mount Shavano
RATING	More difficult
ELEVATION GAIN	4,430 feet, plus 1,080 feet to Tabeguache
ROUND-TRIP DISTANCE	10 miles
ROUND-TRIP TIME	9 to 10 hours
NEAREST TOWN	Poncha Springs

COMMENT: These two Fourteeners are usually climbed together. The US Forest Service and CFI recommend that Shavano be climbed first and Tabeguache (pronounced tab-i-wash) be climbed second.

GETTING THERE: Drive on US 50 west from Salida to Poncha Springs. Go through Poncha Springs and continue west on US 50 for an additional 2 miles to County Road 250. Turn north and follow County Road 250 for 4.8 miles, then bear left onto County Road 252 and continue for approximately another 3 miles to Blanks Gulch Trailhead. The trailhead is at a stone monument that marks the old Blanks Cabin.

THE ROUTE: Walk west up the jeep road for about 100 yards to the intersection with the Colorado Trail, then for 0.3 mile to the intersection with Mount Shavano Trail. Turn west (left). From the Colorado Trail intersection to the saddle just south of Mount Shavano is 3.5 miles. From this point on, the trail is not clearly marked. Follow the ridge to the summit of Mount Shavano, approximately 0.3 mile ahead of you. From the summit of Shavano, descend northwest for .75 mile to the saddle at 13,700 feet, then climb 0.25 mile west to Tabeguache's summit. Return by the same route. Do not try to skirt Shavano's summit since you may end up in McCoy Gulch and in trouble.

Mount Shavano

© 2006 Phil Schmuck

Tabeguache Mountain

© 2006 Phil Schmuck

Capitol Peak

14,130 FEET

MAPS	Capitol Peak 7.5 minute, Trails Illustrated 128–Maroon Bells/Redstone/Marble
RATING	More difficult
ELEVATION GAIN	3,800 feet
ROUND-TRIP DISTANCE	17 miles
ROUND-TRIP TIME	12 hours
NEAREST TOWN	Aspen

COMMENT: Wear a climbing helmet and pack a rope. Watch the weather constantly. The ridge is exposed and lightning storms are frequent from April to September.

GETTING THERE: From Aspen, drive approximately 14 miles toward Glenwood Springs on Colorado 82 until you reach the Conoco station on the left. Turn left (south) and drive almost 2 miles. Keep right at the fork and continue less than 0.5 mile to the next fork. There, keep left. Continue 1.5 mile southwest to another fork. Take the right fork. Follow the road for approximately 4 miles to an area where there are several cabins (in the vicinity of Capitol Creek Guard Station) to the right of the road. Most passenger cars should be able to drive another 1.5 miles to a meadow at 9,400 feet.

THE ROUTE: The Capitol Creek Trail drops 400 feet to the left of the meadow, but a jeep road leaves the upper end of the meadow to Williams Lake and Hardscrabble Lake. At the point where the jeep road crosses a ditch on a bridge, there is a trail that follows the ditch to the left of the road. This trail joins the Capitol Creek Trail without the 400 foot loss in elevation, but you may encounter a problematic stream crossing, especially during runoff, before you can rejoin the trail.

Backpack south from the meadow for 6.5 miles along Capitol Creek Trail to the north end of Capitol Lake at 11,600 feet.

Capitol Peak

© 2006 Phil Schmuck

Camp here. Follow all the Forest Service regulations when you camp since camping rules are enforced vigorously in this area.

From the lake, the Capitol Creek Trail climbs east 0.5 mile to the Capitol-Daly ridge. Drop several hundred feet on the east side of the ridge, and climb up the basin to the point where the ridges on either side merge just before the knife edge. After crossing the knife edge, do an ascending traverse across Capitol's south face, following cairns, to gain the northwest ridge. Follow the ridge to the summit.

SIDEBAR: OH BUDDY, WE CAN MAKE IT.

For reasons not worth discussing, we were late to the mountains, starting a two-mountain route at 10 A.M. The weather looked marginal. We almost trotted up the first peak, arriving exhausted and grumpy at noon. We dropped into the saddle between the two Fourteeners and were almost running toward the next peak. We were absolutely caught up in summit fever. There was only one problem: a thunderstorm was headed right at us.

The next peak was maybe a mile away at most. Some fool said the magic words, "Oh Buddy, we can make it." We went for the next peak and then beat feet back down into the saddle. The sky turned a gray black. There was a moment of real silence and then a blast of wind at maybe forty knots screamed across the saddle. We were stopped in our tracks, huddled together. The wind came harder and harder, and then it went straight up carrying snow pellets with it. We grabbed each other's pack harnesses to stay stable in the wind. And then the sky exploded like tons of explosives going off at once. We were on our knees, trying to survive. We were as scared as we had ever been. Instead of following *A Lightning Protocol* (page 68) we dropped off the ridge and started walking down. We split up so that if we took a lightning strike, it wouldn't kill both of us. One of us said to the other as we split up, "You jerk!"

Capitol Peak

© 2006 Hoffmeyer.com Photography

Snowmass Mountain

14,092 FEET

MAPS	Snowmass Mountain 7.5 minute, Trails Illustrated 128–Maroon Bells/Redstone/Marble
RATING	More difficult or very difficult, depending on route
ELEVATION GAIN	5,700 feet
ROUND-TRIP DISTANCE	22 miles
ROUND-TRIP TIME	16 hours
NEAREST TOWN	Aspen

GETTING THERE: From Aspen, drive approximately 14 miles toward Glenwood Springs on Colorado 82 until you reach the Conoco station on the left. Turn left (south) onto Snowmass Creek Road. After almost 2 miles, at a "T" junction, keep left and continue along Snowmass Creek Road to Snowmass Falls Ranch.

THE ROUTE: Backpack south 9 miles, gaining 2,600 feet in elevation, up Snowmass Creek to Snowmass Lake at 11,000 feet. Camp on the east side of the lake. From this approach the whole of Snowmass Mountain is in view to the right of Hagerman Peak. Hike 0.2 mile around the south shore of the lake and climb west into the basin, keeping to the right (north) of Hagerman Peak. Then, climb onto the ridge between Hagerman and Snowmass and follow the southeast ridge to the summit. This is a moderate but long ascent.

ALTERNATE ROUTE: From Marble, use the 4WD road to Lead King Basin, which is on the way to Crystal. Take a left at a sign marked "Lead King Basin." Park at 9,700 feet where there is also camping. Hike north on an obvious trail to Siberia Lake, passing Geneva and Gem Lakes. Hike east up a steep couloir on the north side of the summit, which is very steep and loose. Do not try to return to Marble via Crystal. The road is very bad.

ELK RANGE

Snowmass Mountain

© 2006 Hoffmeyer.com Photography

North Maroon Peak

14,014 FEET

MAPS	Maroon Bells 7.5 minute, Trails Illustrated 128–Maroon Bells/Redstone/Marble
RATING	Very difficult
ELEVATION GAIN	4,400 feet
ROUND-TRIP DISTANCE	8 miles
ROUND-TRIP TIME	11 hours
NEAREST TOWN	Aspen

COMMENT: The Maroon Bells and Pyramid, which are among Colorado's most picturesque peaks, are also among the most dangerous. The primary hazards of loose and falling rock can be somewhat minimized by climbing in small parties and by going during the week, not on weekends. Wear a helmet and bring a rope.

GETTING THERE: From Aspen, drive northwest 1.2 miles on Colorado 82 and turn left (south). Keep right at the fork that appears immediately on the road to Maroon Lake. Drive about 9 miles to the end of the road. There is a new designated parking lot for climbers. During the summer months, access to Maroon Lake has been restricted to buses and service vehicles.

THE ROUTE: Take the trail past Maroon Lake to Crater Lake (about 1.5 miles), then take the right fork of the trail toward Buckskin Pass. Near timberline (about a mile above Crater Lake), drop to the left of the trail and camp near the stream, at 11,100 feet. From camp, drop west across a gully and stream and climb southwest 0.75 mile to a timberline bench. There is a definite trail across this bench. Pass through a grassy couloir and head southeast to a rock glacier under the north face of North Maroon. Contour south around the east ridge into a second, wide couloir with rocky benches. Climb up this couloir for about 0.3 mile. This will entail climbing through a white band of rock halfway up the distance. There is a cleft in what is otherwise a small cliff. Eventually, this couloir runs into the summit ridge at 13,500 feet. Cross this ridge to the north face. Proceed west to a hard chimney on the north side of the ridge. The chimney can be climbed with a basic amount of technical knowledge. Climb west along the ridge to the summit. Cairns mark this route; alternate trails are more exposed and subject to rock falls.

SIDEBAR: POLYPRO.

We wish we had a dollar for every person we have seen headed up Fourteener trails in shorts and a T-shirt and a water bottle from the jiffy mart. Thousands of folks start that way, and many don't make it very far.

They aren't prepared for the route in a good number of ways, but their worst mistake is the cotton clothing. There is no describing just how cold they will feel in a wet T-shirt with the wind blowing at 12,000 feet.

We're great fans of polypro T-shirts, shirts, vests and jackets. Yes, you are right, polypro can get pretty skanky smelling, but here are the advantages:

- Polypro will keep you warm even when it's wet. If you keep moving in wet polypro you can stay fairly comfortable.
- Polypro dries very quickly. Take your shirt off and shake it in the wind a bit, and it will dry.
- Polypro wicks away sweat from your body.
- Polypro is lighter than wool and more compressible, for the same thickness of insulation.

Maroon (South Maroon) Peak

© 2006 Phil Schmuck

ELK RANGE

North Maroon Peak

© 2006 Phil Schmuck

Maroon (South Maroon) Peak

14,156 FEET

MAPS	Maroon Bells 7.5 minute, Trails Illustrated 128–Maroon Bells/Redstone/Marble
RATING	Very difficult
ELEVATION GAIN	4,400 feet
ROUND-TRIP DISTANCE	10 miles
ROUND-TRIP TIME	12 hours
NEAREST TOWN	Aspen

COMMENT: The Maroon Bells and Pyramid, which are among Colorado's most picturesque peaks, are also among the most dangerous. The primary hazards of loose and falling rock can be somewhat minimized by climbing in small parties and by going during the week, not on weekends. Wear a helmet and bring a rope.

GETTING THERE: From Aspen, drive northwest 1.2 miles on Colorado 82 and turn left (south). Keep right at the fork that appears immediately on the road to Maroon Lake. Drive about 9 miles to the end of the road. There is a new designated parking lot for climbers. During the summer months, access to Maroon Lake has been restricted, mostly to buses and service vehicles.

THE ROUTE: Take the trail past Maroon Lake to Crater Lake, keeping left (not right, as in the North Maroon instructions) at the fork overlooking Crater Lake. Continue approximately 1 mile beyond Crater Lake along the west side of West Maroon Creek to the point where the trail crosses the creek near timberline. Do not cross the creek. Instead, leave the trail and angle southwest, to the right of the stream, up steep, loose, grassy slopes to the ridge. This is a long climb, gaining 2,800 feet. Turn right (north) and follow the ridge to the summit, keeping left (west) where the crest of the ridge is formidable. Much of the route is marked with cairns.

Maroon Bells

© 2006 Hoffmeyer.com Photography

Pyramid Peak

14,018 FEET

MAPS	Maroon Bells 7.5 minute, Trails Illustrated 128–Maroon Bells/Redstone/Marble
RATING	Very difficult
ELEVATION GAIN	4,400 feet
ROUND-TRIP DISTANCE	7 miles
ROUND-TRIP TIME	10 hours
NEAREST TOWN	Aspen

COMMENT: See the comment for the Maroon Bells on previous pages.

GETTING THERE: From Aspen, drive northwest 1.2 miles on Colorado 82 and turn left (south). Keep right at the fork that appears immediately on the road to Maroon Lake. Drive about 9 miles to the end of the road. There is a new designated parking lot for climbers. During the summer months, access to Maroon Lake has been restricted, mostly to buses and service vehicles.

THE ROUTE: Take the trail past Maroon Lake toward Crater Lake. After about 1 mile, you will reach a rocky area marked with a large cairn to the left. Take the trail southeast across a moraine and climb steeply up the trail to the amphitheatre. Once well into the basin, two routes are possible:

For larger parties, the northeast ridge route is better. To follow this route, climb directly out of the basin to the lowest saddle on the east skyline, then keep on the southeast side of the ridge and follow it to the summit.

Smaller groups can proceed from the basin steeply up to the obvious saddle on the northwest ridge of the peak. From there, climb up and south to approach the summit from the south. This route has significant exposure.

Pyramid Peak

© 2006 Phil Schmuck

Castle Peak

14,265 FEET

MAPS	Hayden Peak 7.5 minute, Trails Illustrated 127–Aspen/Independence Pass
RATING	More difficult
ELEVATION GAIN	4,400 feet
ROUND-TRIP DISTANCE	13 miles
ROUND-TRIP TIME	12 hours
NEAREST TOWN	Aspen

COMMENT: This peak is the highest, but also the least difficult to climb, in the Elk Range.

GETTING THERE: From Aspen, drive northwest 1 mile on Colorado 82, then turn left (south) and take an immediate left-hand road to Ashcroft for 12 miles. Continue for 2 miles beyond Ashcroft. Turn right onto the smaller Pearl Pass Road, as the main road continues straight ahead and crosses Castle Creek. After another 0.5 mile, the road starts to climb at 9,900 feet. If using a conventional vehicle, park and camp in the aspen groves.

THE ROUTE: Either hike or use a 4WD vehicle to ascend about 2.5 miles to 11,000 feet, to the Pearl Pass Road junction, which is unmarked. Turn right and follow Montezuma Mine Road to the end, which is well over 12,000 feet.

One route is to climb from the end of the Montezuma Mine Road by heading southwest up the valley. At 13,400 feet, head south to gain the northeast ridge of Castle Peak. Follow the ridge to the summit. Descend by the same route, or descend the northwest ridge to the saddle between Castle Peak and Conundrum Peak. When snow is abundant, a long, exhilarating glissade is possible from Conundrum saddle.

Castle Peak

© 2006 Deborah Atkinson

San Luis Peak

14,014 FEET

MAPS	San Luis Peak 7.5 minute, Stewart Peak 7.5 minute, Trails Illustrated 139–La Garita/Cochetopa Hills
RATING	Moderate
ELEVATION GAIN	3,600 feet
ROUND-TRIP DISTANCE	10 miles
ROUND-TRIP TIME	10 hours
NEAREST TOWN	Gunnison

COMMENT: The challenge in climbing this peak is to reach the Stewart Creek trailhead.

GETTING THERE: Drive 8 miles east of Gunnison on US 50 and turn south on State Road 114 (The Cochetopa Canyon Road). Follow it for 17 miles. Turn right onto Forest Road 3083. The distance from this intersection to the trailhead is about another 30 miles. Pick up these Forest Roads in succession: 3084, 788, 790, 794.28 and 794. A Gunnison Basin Forest Service map is very valuable in finding and following these roads. You can purchase the map at Cimarron Ranger Station, 216 North Colorado, Gunnison, CO 81230, (970-641-0471). Forest Road 794 dead-ends at Stewart Creek—park here. There are numerous campsites in this area.

THE ROUTE: Pick up the trailhead at the dead end of the road and hike west up Stewart Creek Valley, keeping to the right (north) side of the creek most of the time. The trail is easily discernable. At the end of the valley you will see a high, flattened, pyramid-shaped peak. After climbing past several gulches coming in from the left, ascend to the saddle on the northwest slope of San Luis Peak. From this point, the summit can be seen 0.2 mile away in a west, southwest direction, but this is still a long hike.

San Luis Peak

© 2006 PhIL Schmuck

Uncompahgre Peak

14,309 FEET

MAPS	Uncompahgre Peak 7.5 minute, Trails Illustrated 141–Telluride/Silverton/ Ouray/Lake City
RATING	More difficult
ELEVATION GAIN	3,900 feet
ROUND-TRIP DISTANCE	11 miles
ROUND-TRIP TIME	9 hours
NEAREST TOWN	Lake City

COMMENT: Uncompahgre and Wetterhorn are sometimes climbed in one day; however, the Nellie Creek route is strongly recommended. If climbing Uncompahgre from Matterhorn Basin, it is important to stay on the established trail all the way to the summit, due to the sensitivity of the alpine environment on Uncompahgre.

GETTING THERE: In Lake City, find County Road 20 and drive west for about 5 miles. Turn north (right) onto the Nellie Creek Road. This road is not recommended for a passenger car. The road has steep switchbacks and can be slippery during wet weather. A 4WD vehicle is advisable. Park at the end of the road.

THE ROUTE: The Nellie Creek trail is well traveled and easy to follow as it goes west to the southeast ridge of Uncompahgre, and then north up to the summit.

SIDEBAR: THE REST STEP.

There are a number of theories about the most efficient way to hike a Fourteener. Here's what works for us. It's an old mountaineering trick called the "Rest Step" where you move one foot upward, pause, take a breath, move your other foot up next to the uphill foot, pause, take a breath, then move that foot uphill and pause, and take a breath. It's slow, but when your lungs are screaming for oxygen, it works.

Uncompahgre Peak

© 2006 Phil Schmuck

Wetterhorn Peak

14,015 FEET

MAPS	Wetterhorn Peak 7.5 minute, Trails Illustrated 141–Telluride/Silverton/ Ouray/Lake City
RATING	More difficult
ELEVATION GAIN	3,600 feet
ROUND-TRIP DISTANCE	8 miles
ROUND-TRIP TIME	7 hours
NEAREST TOWN	Lake City

GETTING THERE: From Lake City, pick up Henson Creek Road (look for the Engineer Pass sign) and drive 10 miles west and 1.5 miles northwest to a campground near Matterhorn Creek at 10,400 feet. The road is permanently closed to vehicles a short distance above camp.

THE ROUTE: Hike north along the Ridgestock Driveway to the junction with the Wetterhorn Peak Trail. This junction is marked with a sign. Follow the established trail across Matterhorn Basin to the summit ridgeline. Work up the west side of the peak to the summit on a system of ledges. The route appears to be steep and formidable, but it goes well if the route is dry.

WETTERHORN AND UMCOMPAHGRE TOGETHER: If climbing Uncompahgre from Matterhorn Basin, it is important to stay on the established trail all the way to the summit, due to the sensitivity of the alpine environment on Uncompahgre. This is a very long climb.

SIDEBAR: WATER.

We got lost and spent hours in an endless talus field on a hot day. We climbed a false summit. We ran out of water on the real summit. We were very dry when we got to the car. Carry more water than you think you will need. You have been warned.

Wetterhorn Peak

© 2006 Deborah Atkinson

Redcloud Peak
Sunshine Peak

14,034 FEET

14,001 FEET

MAPS	Redcloud Peak 7.5 minute, Trails Illustrated 141–Telluride/Silverton/Ouray/Lake City
RATING	More difficult
ELEVATION GAIN	3,600 feet, plus 500 feet
ROUND-TRIP DISTANCE	8 miles
ROUND-TRIP TIME	8 hours
NEAREST TOWN	Lake City

COMMENT: Redcloud and Sunshine are traditionally done together.

GETTING THERE: From Lake City, drive approximately 15 miles up the Lake Fork of the Gunnison River on County Road 30. Take the right-hand fork onto County Road 4 toward Cinnamon Pass and drive for just over 4 miles to Grizzly Creek at 10,400 feet. There is an excellent campsite near Grizzly Gulch in the area of Silver Creek with water (not potable) and an outhouse.

THE ROUTE: Using the standard cairn route, hike northeast up the trail 2 miles to the northwest side of Silver Creek. Continue on the trail along the creek. At timberline, cross the creek, gain the saddle north of Redcloud, and climb the ridge southeast for 1 mile to the summit of Redcloud.

To Sunshine, follow the Redcloud ridge south 1.5 miles. You will drop 500 feet between peaks. Return over Redcloud. In the saddle between Redcloud and Sunshine Peaks there is an apparent "descent" into the South Fork drainage that looks very inviting. It is steep, dangerous and contains tricky talus. Once you take this wrong trail, it is extremely difficult to retrace your steps back to the saddle to access the safer route.

Redcloud Peak

© 2006 Phil Schmuck

Sunshine Peak

© 2006 Phil Schmuck

Handies Peak

14,048 FEET

MAPS	Handies Peak 7.5 minute, Redcloud 7.5 minute, Trails Illustrated 141–Telluride/Silverton/Ouray/Lake City
RATING	Moderate
ELEVATION GAIN	3,600 feet
ROUND-TRIP DISTANCE	7 miles
ROUND-TRIP TIME	5 hours
NEAREST TOWN	Lake City

GETTING THERE: From Lake City, drive approximately 15 miles up the Lake Fork of the Gunnison River on County Road 30. Take the right-hand fork onto County Road 4 toward Cinnamon Pass and drive for just over 4 miles to Grizzly Creek at 10,400 feet. There is an excellent campsite near Grizzly Gulch in the area of Silver Creek with water (not potable) and an outhouse.

THE ROUTE: Cross the Lake Fork of the Gunnison River, and hike up the Grizzly Gulch Trail north out of the valley and west to the ridge. From the ridge it is an easy climb south to the summit.

ALTERNATE ROUTE: An easier 4- to 5-hour round-trip climb, that has an elevation gain of only 2,700 feet, is possible from the American Basin. Continue south on Cinnamon Pass Road for about 3.5 miles past Grizzly Creek. Take a 4WD road heading south into American Basin. Park along this road. Follow the road as it changes into a trail and begins to climb up grassy slopes. Continue south and west to the south ridge of Handies, then to the summit. Return by the same route, following the trail.

Handies Peak

© 2006 Phil Schmuck

Windom Peak

14,082 FEET

MAPS	Mountain View Crest 7.5 minute, Columbine Pass 7.5 minute, Storm King Peak 7.5 minute, Trails Illustrated 140– Weminuche Wilderness
RATING	Very difficult
ELEVATION GAIN	2,600 feet
ROUND-TRIP DISTANCE	3 miles
ROUND-TRIP TIME	5 hours
NEAREST TOWN	Durango

COMMENT: Windom and Sunlight are close together, with little elevation loss on the route connecting them. They should be climbed on the same day, unless weather dictates otherwise. Mount Eolus can also be climbed from the same high camp. Carrying a rope is a good idea.

GETTING THERE: To reach the trailhead take the Durango and Silverton Railroad from Durango. Call early for reservations: 970-247-2733. When you disembark at Needleton, cross the river on the suspension bridge and backpack east 7.2 miles up the trail along Needle Creek. Camp in Chicago Basin at about 11,000 feet, in the area where the trail crosses to the south bank of Needle Creek and starts up Columbine Pass.

THE ROUTE: Follow Needle Creek and the good trail north 1 mile to Twin Lakes at 12,500 feet. Turn east up the large basin between Sunlight and Windom. Keep to the left of Peak 18 (13,472), the dominant feature on the ascent. Continue east 0.2 mile and climb southeast to the west ridge of Windom at 13,250 feet, near the Peak 18-Windom Peak col, a depression in the crest of the ridge. Continue east along the ridge for 0.2 mile to the summit.

Windom Peak

© 2006 Phil Schmuck

Sunlight Peak

14,059 FEET

MAPS	Mountain View Crest 7.5, Trails Illustrated 140–Weminuche Wilderness
RATING	Very difficult
ELEVATION GAIN	2,700 feet
ROUND-TRIP DISTANCE	3 miles
ROUND-TRIP TIME	5 hours
NEAREST TOWN	Durango

GETTING THERE: To reach the trailhead take the Durango and Silverton Railroad from Durango. Call early for reservations: 970-247-2733. When you disembark at Needleton, cross the river on the suspension bridge and backpack east 7.2 miles up the trail along Needle Creek. Camp in Chicago Basin at about 11,000 feet, in the area where the trail crosses to the south bank of Needle Creek and starts up Columbine Pass.

THE ROUTE: From Chicago Basin, follow the trail north to Twin Lakes. Turn east into the basin between Sunlight and Peak 13,995. Climb gradually up to the connecting ridge between Sunlight and Windom. Turn north (left) to Sunlight Peak. You will traverse the northwest shoulder of Peak 13,995. Then continue northwest up Sunlight's ridge to the summit. A rope is recommended for anyone climbing the last 10 feet to the true summit. It is a long way down to the north.

SIDEBAR: TWOFERS.

A number of Fourteeners are easily done together, including Grays and Torreys in the Front Range; Blanca and Ellingwood in the Sangre de Cristo Range. In the Sawatch Range, Belford and Oxford are done together as are Harvard and Columbia, and Shavano and Tabeguache. Redcloud and Sunshine are done together in the San Juan Range as well as Windom and Sunlight.

Sunlight Peak

© 2006 Phil Schmuck

Mount Eolus

14,083 FEET

MAPS	Mountain View Crest 7.5 minute, Columbine Pass 7.5 minute, Storm King Peak 7.5 minute, Trails Illustrated 140– Weminuche Wilderness
RATING	Very difficult
ELEVATION GAIN	2,800 feet
ROUND-TRIP DISTANCE	6 miles
ROUND-TRIP TIME	8 hours
NEAREST TOWN	Durango

COMMENT: Mount Eolus can be climbed from the same Chicago Basin high camp that you use for Windom and Sunshine.

GETTING THERE: To reach the trailhead take the Durango and Silverton Railroad from Durango. Call early for reservations: 970-247-2733. When you disembark at Needleton, cross the river on the suspension bridge and backpack east 7.2 miles up the trail along Needle Creek. Camp in Chicago Basin at about 11,000 feet, in the area where the trail crosses to the south bank of Needle Creek and starts up Columbine Pass.

THE ROUTE: From Chicago Basin, follow the trail north to Twin Lakes. Before you get to Twin Lakes, head west. As you approach the great east face of Eolus, head northeast up a slab to the saddle between Eolus and Glacier Point at 13,700 feet. Turn west to the saddle between Eolus and North Eolus. Traverse southwest across a narrow and exposed ridge that enjoys the names, "Sidewalk in the Sky" and "Catwalk." The ridge terminates in the east face of Eolus. Use the ledges on the face, keeping to the left and taking care to select the route, to ascend to the summit.

Mount Eolus

© 2006 Hoffmeyer.com Photography

Mount Sneffels

14,150 FEET

MAPS	Mount Sneffels 7.5 minute, Telluride 7.5 minute, Trails Illustrated 141–Telluride/Silverton/Ouray/Lake City
RATING	More difficult
ELEVATION GAIN	3,400 feet
ROUND-TRIP DISTANCE	6 miles
ROUND-TRIP TIME	5 to 6 hours
NEAREST TOWN	Ouray

GETTING THERE: From US 550, 0.5 mile south of Ouray, turn right and drive 6.5 miles. The Yankee Boy Basin Road bears to the right all the way to its end. Drive to timberline and park.

THE ROUTE: Follow the Yankee Boy Basin Road up Yankee Boy Basin—famous for its alpine wildflowers and humming-birds—to its end, then pick up the Blue Lake Pass Trail. Follow this trail to 12,700 feet, then head northwest on the established trail, traversing around a boulder field to gain a wide couloir. The couloir leads to a saddle at 13,500 feet. Turn northwest on the saddle and enter a narrower and steeper rock-filled couloir that leads up to the wall under the summit. Before reaching the end of this couloir, look for another much smaller and shorter couloir, and take it. It leads to the left and terminates in a V-shaped notch through which you can climb out onto the approach to the summit, about a 100 yards above.

If either of these couloirs become too difficult because of snow, it may be possible to move to the west and approach the summit across the southwest face of Sneffels.

Mount Sneffels

© 2006 Phil Schmuck

Wilson Peak

14,017 FEET

MAPS	Little Cone 7.5 minute, Gray Head 7.5 minute, Delores Peak 7.5 minute, Mount Wilson 7.5 minute, Trails Illustrated 141–Telluride/Silverton/Ouray/Lake City
RATING	Very difficult
ELEVATION GAIN	3,350 feet
ROUND-TRIP DISTANCE	6 miles
ROUND-TRIP TIME	10 hours
NEAREST TOWN	Placerville

COMMENT: Until further notice, private land parcels in Silver Pick Basin and near Wilson Peak have been closed to public access by the landowner. This private land closure begins approximately 1 mile south of the Silver Pick trailhead and parking lot. Although all National Forest lands surrounding the private land remain open to public use, this private land closure restricts all traditional access routes to the Rock of Ages Saddle through Silver Pick Basin, and closes public access on the standard route (southwest ridge) to Wilson Peak.

GETTING THERE: From Placerville, drive 7 miles southeast to Vanadium on Colorado 145. Turn right up Big Bear Creek. At 2.5 miles south of Vanadium, keep right. At 4 miles, take the center choice of three roads. At about 6 miles, the road is blocked to further vehicle travel.

THE ROUTE: It is still legal to climb Wilson Peak via the West Face route. Silver Pick Road is open to the public for 0.9 mile from this trailhead gate. You may access Silver Pick Basin by leaving the road before the private property claims begin. Stay on the north side of the basin and link existing trails where possible. Avoid the rock house ruins and Rock of Ages saddle areas.

Wilson Peak

© 2006 Deborah Atkinson

Mount Wilson

14,246 FEET

MAPS	Gray Head 7.5 minute, Delores Peak 7.5 minute, Trails Illustrated 141–Telluride/Silverton/Ouray/Lake City
RATING	Very difficult
ELEVATION GAIN	5,200 feet
ROUND-TRIP DISTANCE	15 miles
ROUND-TRIP TIME	15 hours
NEAREST TOWN	Telluride and Rico

COMMENT: A climbing helmet and rope are advisable for this route, and bring an ice axe early in the season. Using the Kilpacker Creek approach, Mount Wilson and El Diente can be done in the same day by a strong party.

GETTING THERE: To approach Mount Wilson from Navajo Basin, drive south on Colorado 145 for 5.5 miles beyond Lizard Head Pass. Turn right (west) on Dunton Road (Forest Road 535). Follow Dunton Road for 6 miles, past Morgan Camp, to Forest Road 207. Then turn right for 0.2 mile on a short road that terminates in a parking area at West Dolores River. The Navajo Lake trailhead is located at the northern end of the parking area. Follow the trail north along the river for 5 miles to Navajo Lake, where there are campsites east of the lake.

THE ROUTE: Climb east to the head of Navajo Basin. At 12,300 feet, turn south and follow the ridge on the western side between Gladstone and Mount Wilson. This should enable you to skirt the permanent snowfield along the way. At 13,800 feet, head southwest to gain the northeast ridge of Mount Wilson. At 14,100 feet, head south through a notch in the ridge. This leads to a dramatic, exposed ridge that culminates in the summit. Descend using the same route.

Mount Wilson

© 2006 Phil Schmuck

El Diente

14,159 FEET

MAPS	Delores Peak 7.5 minute, Mount Wilson 7.5 minute, Trails Illustrated 141–Telluride/Silverton/Ouray/Lake City
RATING	Very difficult
ELEVATION GAIN	4,100 feet
ROUND-TRIP DISTANCE	13 miles
ROUND-TRIP TIME	12 hours
NEAREST TOWN	Telluride

COMMENT: This is a difficult, dangerous and challenging climb. It is strongly advised that you consult more detailed guides and carry the appropriate maps and equipment. A climbing helmet and rope are advisable for this route, and bring an ice axe early in the season.

GETTING THERE: From Telluride, drive on Colorado 145 east, then south over Lizard Head Pass until you reach Dunton Road. After about 5.5 miles, as Dunton Road begins to lose altitude, turn right onto a small road that passes through a meadow. Continue for another 0.25 mile to a grove of trees where there is limited parking.

THE ROUTE: Hike on a closed jeep road north and northeast for 1.5 miles to Kilpacker Creek. Do not cross the creek. Just south of the creek, pick up a trail heading east and continue generally up along the creek after the trail crosses the creek and ends. Pass two waterfalls near timberline. Continue up the drainage to gain the Mount Wilson-El Diente ridge. Gain the ridge to the left, or west, of a formation called Organ Pipes. This route eliminates a difficult traverse around the formation. As you head for the summit, switch to the north side of the ridge.

El Diente

© 2006 Phil Schmuck

Glossary

BASIN: a symmetrically-dipping, elongated, circular flat area.

CAIRN: a pile of rocks, usually built by humans to mark a trail.

COL: a small pass between two peaks.

CONTOUR: to traverse generally at the same elevation or slightly up or down.

CORNICE: an overhanging edge of snow on a ridge.

COULOIR: a steep gully or gorge frequently filled with snow or ice.

EXPOSURE: the empty space below a climber, the distance a climber would fall before doing a grounder.

GLISSADE: a usually voluntary act of sliding down a steep slope.

GOATHEAD: any climber who says, "Oh Buddy, we can make it," and pushes on in front of a thunderstorm.

GULCH: a deep V-shaped valley formed by erosion.

MORAINE: sheets of rock debris transported by glaciers or ice sheets.

PARIAH: any self-absorbed amateur who cuts across switchbacks.

POST HOLE: the art of repeatedly breaking through crusty snow, often up to the climber's waist.

SADDLE: a high pass between two peaks, larger than a col.

SCREE: loose, broken, unstable rock that climbers can never avoid.

SLAB: a relatively flat and featureless block of rock.

TALUS: (see scree)

TUNDRA: treeless area where the dominant vegetation is grasses, mosses, and lichens.

Colorado Fourteeners Ranked by Height

MOUNTAIN	PAGE	ALTITUDE	RANGE
1. Mount Elbert	56	14,433	Sawatch
2. Mount Massive	54	14,421	Sawatch
3. Mount Harvard	66	14,420	Sawatch
4. Blanca Peak	40	14,345	Sangre de Cristo
5. La Plata Peak	58	14,336	Sawatch
6. Uncompahgre Peak	94	14,309	San Juan
7. Crestone Peak	32	14,294	Sangre de Cristo
8. Mount Lincoln	46	14,286	Mosquito
9. Grays Peak	18	14,270	Front
10. Mount Antero	72	14,269	Sawatch
11. Torreys Peak	18	14,267	Front
12. Castle Peak	90	14,265	Elk
13. Quandry Peak	44	14,265	Mosquito
14. Mount Evans	22	14,264	Front
15. Longs Peak	16	14,255	Front
16. Mount Wilson	112	14,246	San Juan
17. Mount Shavano	74	14,229	Sawatch
18. Mount Princeton	70	14,197	Sawatch
19. Mount Belford	60	14,197	Sawatch
20. Crestone Needle	34	14,197	Sangre de Cristo
21. Mount Yale	68	14,196	Sawatch
22. Mount Bross	46	14,172	Mosquito
23. Kit Carson Peak	28	14,165	Sangre de Cristo
24. El Diente	114	14,159	San Juan
25. Maroon (South Maroon) Peak	86	14,156	Elk

MOUNTAIN	PAGE	ALTITUDE	RANGE
26. Tabeguache Mountain	74	14,155	Sawatch
27. Mount Oxford	60	14,153	Sawatch
28. Mount Sneffels	108	14,150	San Juan
29. Mount Democrat	46	14,148	Mosquito
30. Capitol Peak	76	14,130	Elk
31. Pikes Peak	26	14,110	Front
32. Snowmass Mountain	80	14,092	Elk
33. Mount Eolus	106	14,083	San Juan
34. Windom Peak	102	14,082	San Juan
35. Mount Columbia	66	14,073	Sawatch
36. Missouri Mountain	62	14,067	Sawatch
37. Humboldt Peak	30	14,064	Sangre de Cristo
38. Mount Bierstadt	24	14,060	Front
39. Sunlight Peak	104	14,059	San Juan
40. Handies Peak	100	14,048	San Juan
41. Culebra Peak	42	14,047	Sangre de Cristo
42. Mount Lindsey	36	14,042	Sangre de Cristo
43. Ellingwood Peak	40	14,042	Sangre de Cristo
44. Little Bear Peak	38	14,037	Sangre de Cristo
45. Mount Sherman	50	14,036	Mosquito
46. Redcloud Peak	98	14,034	San Juan
47. Pyramid Peak	88	14,018	Elk
48. Wilson Peak	110	14,017	San Juan
49. Wetterhorn Peak	96	14,015	San Juan
50. North Maroon Peak	82	14,014	Elk
51. San Luis Peak	92	14,014	San Juan
52. Mount of the Holy Cross	52	14,005	Sawatch
53. Huron Peak	64	14,003	Sawatch
54. Sunshine Peak	98	14,001	San Juan

Colorado Fourteeners Climbing Tick List

MOUNTAIN	PAGE	CLIMBING PARTNER	DATE
Longs Peak	16		
Grays Peak	18		
Torreys Peak	18		
Mount Evans	22		
Mount Bierstadt	24		
Pikes Peak	26		
Kit Carson Peak	28		
Humboldt Peak	30		
Crestone Peak	32		
Crestone Needle	34		
Mount Lindsey	36		
Little Bear Peak	38		
Blanca Peak	40		
Ellingwood Peak	40		
Culebra Peak	42		
Quandry Peak	44		
Mount Lincoln	46		
Mount Democrat	46		
Mount Bross	46		
Mount Sherman	50		
Mount of the Holy Cross	52		
Mount Massive	54		
Mount Elbert	56		
La Plata Peak	58		
Mount Belford	60		

MOUNTAIN	PAGE	CLIMBING PARTNER	DATE
Mount Oxford	60		
Missouri Mountain	62		
Huron Peak	64		
Mount Harvard	66		
Mount Columbia	66		
Mount Yale	68		
Mount Princeton	70		
Mount Antero	72		
Mount Shavano	74		
Tabeguache Mountain	74		
Capitol Peak	76		
Snowmass Mountain	80		
North Maroon Peak	82		
Maroon (South Maroon) Peak	86		
Pyramid Peak	88		
Castle Peak	90		
San Luis Peak	92		
Uncompahgre Peak	94		
Wetterhorn Peak	96		
Redcloud Peak	98		
Sunshine Peak	98		
Handies Peak	100		
Windom Peak	102		
Sunlight Peak	104		
Mount Eolus	106		
Mount Sneffels	108		
Wilson Peak	110		
Mount Wilson	112		
El Diente	114		

Y IN ASHF

CW00746156

AQUARIUS

20th January – 18th February

An argument with someone you love brings trouble crashing down like a bolt from the blue. Be brave. You are not helpless and must trust your Aquarian independence to get you out of your tight spot.

0 749 718 862 837 02

MARIA PALMER

HORRORSCOPES

AQUARIUS

TRAPPED

Nottinghamshire County Council

P53003837

Leisure Services / Libraries

MAMMOTH

First published in Great Britain 1995
by Mammoth, an imprint of Reed Consumer Books Ltd
Michelin House, 81 Fulham Road, London SW3 6RB
and Auckland, Melbourne, Singapore and Toronto

Copyright © Alick Rowe, 1995

Horroscopes is a trademark of Reed International Books Ltd

The right of Alick Rowe to be identified as author of this
work has been asserted by him in accordance with
the Copyright, Designs and Patents Act 1988

ISBN 0 7497 1886 2

A CIP catalogue record for this title
is available from the British Library

Printed in Great Britain
by BPC Paperbacks

This paperback is sold subject to the condition
that it shall not, by way of trade or otherwise,
be lent, resold, hired out, or otherwise circulated
without the publisher's prior consent in any form
of binding or cover other than that in which
it is published and without a similar condition
including this condition being imposed
on the subsequent purchaser.

ONE

Alan and Lucy Graham sat as far away from each other as the small room would allow. It had been a bad day for the whole family.

'You always stick up for Dad,' Lucy complained, pulling her head back from the half-open window and flicking ash from the end of her cigarette outside.

Alan shouted back, 'So what? You always stick up for Mum.'

The strengthening February wind outside blew back the flakes of ash. Michael Penn grinned annoyingly from the carpet where he was playing a computer game. 'Now, now, children,' he said. 'If you're going to smoke, drink *and* argue about your boring parents I'm going.'

'Who's keeping you!' muttered Lucy. Neither of them liked Michael.

'Can't you shut the window?' Alan moaned. 'It's cold enough in the house without you letting the warmth out.'

Lucy threw the rest of the cigarette out and slammed down the window as hard as she could. 'You make me sick,' she hissed, striding to the door.

Michael handed the can of beer to Alan who took a heavy swig. He didn't much like beer. He guessed that Lucy didn't enjoy cigarettes either. It seemed to be what the Graham twins did whenever they were fed up and their parents were out of the house – he stole one of his father's cans from the fridge and Lucy took a cigarette from behind the cookery books in the kitchen where their mother hid her secret stock. He passed the can back to Michael and gazed through the window. A hundred metres away, Archenford Cathedral rose, massive and floodlit in the stormy night. It was always impressive. He just wished Dad liked living in the close as much as Mum seemed to. Or perhaps it was just another excuse for arguing. That's all they seemed to do now. All four of them.

Michael broke into his thoughts. 'Do you want to play another?'

Alan shook his head. He knew that Michael had only called in to show off his new game. He wondered where Michael got the money. His father worked in the cathedral office, his mother managed the souvenir shop and, although Michael did a paper round, it seemed too little to account for the expensive novelties he paraded in front of the other children living in the cathedral close. That was one of the problems about living in the close: you were part of a small community and couldn't escape the others.

'What time's your mother coming back?' Michael asked, getting to his feet and packing away the cassette in a plastic bag.

Alan shrugged. 'Late. About one. Whenever *your* mother throws her out.'

Michael grinned irritatingly again. 'That won't be for a long time. My dad's away tonight and you know what your mother's like when she gets together with mine.' He punched Alan jokily on the arm. 'Particularly when naughty Alan and Lucy have been upsetting her.'

'Shut up, Michael,' Alan said sharply, following the boy into the hall where Lucy was checking the contents of her overnight case.

'Goodnight, Lucy,' Michael said in a silly singsong voice as he pulled on his anorak. 'I don't envy you. It's going to be really bad on the downs tonight.'

Alan opened the door and the wind gusted in, rattling pictures on the wall and blowing letters from the shelf.

'Remember to take water wings and an anchor,' Michael shouted against the storm.

'See you, Michael,' Alan shouted back and slammed the door shut.

'That boy is a total dickhead,' Lucy muttered.

Alan put back the envelopes. 'Sure is,' he said, trying a smile.

Lucy sensed the peace-offering and took it. 'He's probably right about the water wings and anchor,' she replied.

Alan looked up at the clock. 'About an hour before they come for us.' He collected the empty beer can from the living room and crossed to the kitchen door. 'Should be a good laugh,' he called.

'At least it'll get us out of this rotten house,' Lucy replied.

Alan nodded as he flipped the can into the waste bin. That was a problem with winter; everybody was shut in – living on top of each other. When adults were arguing, shouting, coldly sarcastic with each other, the children couldn't ignore it. Alan flipped the lid of the bin shut with his toe. Beer and cigarettes. Adult things. He couldn't imagine why he and Lucy should want to copy adults when adults were being so bloodyminded.

Lucy came in. 'Want a coffee?' She knew what his answer would be and filled the kettle without waiting. Alan reached for two mugs and the coffee. They were looking forward to their adventure. Friends from school, Dawn and Lawrence Vaughan, had invited them to their farm for the weekend. The Vaughans lived about ten miles away, high on the Broomyard Downs. In this wild weather it should be something to remember. It was exciting to be going away late at night too; the Vaughans were collecting their youngest son from a concert in Broomyard before leaving for Archenford.

Lucy opened a new carton of milk. 'Do you suppose Mother's all right?' she asked. Lucy felt guilty. The plan had been for Cathy Graham to greet the Vaughans and give them a drink before they set out for the downs but there had been a nasty argument between Alan and Mum – about Dad, of course. Instead of trying to cool it down Lucy had joined in on Alan's side and ten seconds

4

later the slammed door had announced that their mother had had enough. Her friend Sara – Michael's mother – had phoned later to tell them, rather coldly, that Cathy needed a little time and space of her own and, since they had made it obvious that they didn't need her, they had better give the Vaughans a drink themselves. They could lock the door behind them when they left. Lucy and Alan hated Sara as much as they hated her son.

'Anyway, it's better that Mum and Dad have the place to themselves when he gets home,' Lucy murmured as she flicked through a magazine waiting for the water to boil. The phone rang and Alan went to answer it.

Jamie Graham separated from the rest of his squadron over Wiltshire and immediately relaxed. He liked flying independently of the other pilots. Now there was just him and his superb Jaguar airplane – a previous pilot had christened it *Lightning* and painted a suitably macho bolt of lightning below the cockpit. He glimpsed lights through a gap in the clouds – Devizes – and checked his course towards Bristol. *Lightning* was buffeted by a sudden squall and Jamie grunted. The change in weather had been forecast but not so early. He wondered what his wife and children were doing. It had been a bad day; it couldn't go on like this.

Lucy and Alan sipped their coffee and decided not to tell their mother. They knew when she heard that the Vaughans' Land-rover had side-slipped into a ditch and couldn't be recovered until tomorrow she would want to come home at once.

'Will Dad ever live here again?' Lucy looked over the table at Alan and shrugged. For the last week Jamie had been living in the officers' mess at RAF Meeston. 'Why are they so fed up with each other all of a sudden?' she persisted. Alan got up from the table and stretched. He ambled across to the cathedral calendar on the wall and crossed out 'Broomfield – Vaughans'.

'What can we do about it anyway?' his sister sighed. 'Nothing.'

Alan was not so sure. He was screwing up his eyes to read the tiny printing. 'Tomorrow's the feast-day of Rycharde.'

Lucy looked over. 'So?'

Alan came to the table, excited. 'You remember Gran – when she nearly died.'

Lucy remembered. Dad's mother had been very ill and one of the vergers had suggested that secretly saying a prayer and lighting a candle at the shrine of the medieval patron saint of Archenford might help. Gran had recovered and Alan had been very impressed. Lucy could see Alan was becoming more enthusiastic. 'What about Mother?' she asked cautiously.

'No problem! We'll be back by one.'

Lucy stood up and fixed Alan with one of her pitying looks. 'You mean now? Light a candle now?'

Alan was already leaving the room. 'Not

exactly now,' he called back. 'At midnight. I'll get Mum's keys.'

Lucy was not happy about this. She knew their mother would go crazy if she knew her children had borrowed her keys. She hurried from the kitchen after Alan. 'Alan – we can't.'

He hurried from their mother's small study waving her keys triumphantly. 'Oh yes, we can.'

He saw her unease and made himself calm down. 'Look,' he said simply, 'Mum and Dad are in trouble. I know you don't believe in things like this as much as I do but I want to help them. And just now this is the only thing I can think of.' He watched her uncertain face. 'You don't have to come,' he said cruelly. 'I can probably do it better on my own.'

Cathy Graham looked at the clock over her friend's mantelpiece and decided she had better make for home, even though it was early. She waited patiently while Sara laid out the cards one last time. 'I must go soon,' she said, grateful to her friend for listening to her troubles but needing to do some hard thinking on her own. She didn't have much faith in tarot cards. Sara looked up. 'Just let's see what fortune's bringing you.'

Cathy smiled and finished her cup of coffee. 'Thanks for listening,' she said. 'I didn't mean to bore you to death. I just didn't know who else I could talk to. You know what this town is like for gossip.'

Sara snapped over the central card. It showed a tall stone tower hit by a jagged bolt of lightning.

7

Flames burned at the tiny windows and, beneath the impact, a man and woman were flying through the air. 'The Tower Struck by Lightning,' Sara murmured.

Cathy raised her eyebrows. 'Lightning? That's what they call Jamie's plane.'

'I know,' her friend murmured, sweeping all the cards up into a pack.

'Where's Michael tonight?' Cathy asked as she pulled on her coat.

Sara smiled. 'Oh, you know Michael. He could be anywhere. I don't worry about him.' She opened the door and a sudden gust tugged hard at it.

Cathy looked past the yellow streetlights up to the stormy sky. 'Jamie's flying tonight,' she said quietly. She did up her coat wondering how long it would be before the children began to realise their father preferred living on the base to being at home.

'Penny for your thoughts,' grinned Sara.

Cathy smiled. 'They're not worth it.'

The first sleet scattered across the road and the two friends squealed comically. 'Hope the kids don't get blown away at Broomyard,' Sara shouted. 'Sooner them than me!' She waved and closed the door.

'This is a stupid idea,' muttered Lucy as she closed the heavy door behind them.

'Lock it,' hissed Alan and she did, though she didn't know why. Alan was already pressing ahead and she hurried to catch him up, shivering.

The orange floodlighting, which bathed the outside of the cathedral, made the inside seem even more strange and cavernous than during the day. There was a booming noise as the wind slapped against the tower high above them and Lucy regretted being talked – yet again – into one of Alan's hare-brained schemes.

'What's the time?' whispered Alan as they made for the door that led down to the chapel where Rycharde's shrine stood.

'I don't know,' she whispered back. 'It must be getting on for midnight.'

Neither knew why they should feel the need to whisper; there was nobody to hear them.

It was a strange feeling to be alone in the cathedral, making for the shrine of a saint with a candle to light at midnight as his feast-day began.

'Keep up with me,' Alan hissed anxiously. 'Are you scared?'

Lucy moved up to his side. 'Of course not,' she lied. The wind hit the high square tower again and the booming echoed once more through the vast emptiness. Alan felt very uneasy; he wished he had let Lucy talk him out of it.

'Come on,' Lucy said angrily. 'If we've got to go through with this mad scheme of yours, we've got to be down there when the clock strikes.'

Twenty miles away, *Lightning* staggered in the sky and Jamie whistled quietly. He was rocketing towards the border now, where Herefordshire gave way to Archenford and was already in

9

contact with Meeston Air Traffic Control who had warned of worse weather ahead and offered him the chance to divert to another airfield a hundred and sixty miles away. Jamie was tired and wanted to be home; he and Cathy had important things to talk about. Since he couldn't climb above the storm he decided to lose height and try to find calmer conditions there. He didn't tell the controller because he knew he would forbid it. Too noisy for sleepers on the ground. Less safe for the pilot in the sky.

Alan and Lucy hurried past a row of ancient tombs. Outside the cathedral the wind was thrashing the trees so that shadows danced and waved across the paving stones, matching the antics of the wind as it smashed and howled through the branches in the close. They came to the door which led down to the Shrine Chapel and the other underground room, the ancient treasury. Alan stood aside while Lucy fumbled for the right key. Her mother would kill them if she ever knew about this, she thought. When they had passed through – and locked it behind them, just to be safe – the exterior sounds became a distant dull groaning. They were in the oldest part of the building now where columns and walls were thicker. No light came from outside and Alan had just switched on his torch when they heard the clock mechanism begin to wind up for the midnight chimes seventy metres above them in the tower.

'Quickly,' cried Alan as Lucy found the key to

the shrine door and turned the old-fashioned lock.

The first emergency warning light began flashing as Jamie's Jaguar ripped low through the stormy sky above Broomyard, waking the Vaughans and scaring their animals. Two more lights came on the other side of the cockpit. Jamie had never had three emergency lights at one time. As the controller demanded more information Jamie checked the dials and felt his heart jump. Too low – far too low. He rocketed out of low cloud to see street lights. There was a sudden dip in engine power and the nose dropped before he could power the engine back to screaming pitch. Jamie struggled to haul the machine up again, frantically searching for the guiding landmark of the cathedral. He saw it. It was floodlit. Thank God. He boosted engine power even further and the airplane began to pull away towards the darkness beyond the streetlights – but very slowly.

Cathy hurried into the close just as, seventy metres above, high in the tower, the huge ancient bell that would ring out the twelve midnight strokes began to move. There were seven other bells in the dark bell-tower but one was seldom used. All the bell-ringers regarded it with a sort of dread respect. The Black Sergeant had been cast, in 1565, in Archenford itself. The massive bell had a solemn inscription carved deep in the iron: YE FOR WHOM I CALLE SHAL

11

HEARE MEE NEVERE. The Black Sergeant rang out only to announce the death of a priest of Archenford Cathedral and only the most senior bell-ringer was permitted to toll it.

With a sick despair Jamie knew the Jaguar was going down and that he must eject in the next few seconds. He fixed all his concentration on the floodlit spire as he fought to turn the Jaguar's nose towards the safe fields to the south. High in the cathedral tower, as midnight began to strike, the bell swung smoothly down and the timer controlling the floodlighting automatically cut out. There was suddenly no cathedral. Jamie shouted helplessly and had a sudden vision of his children who – at this very moment – would be below him, in terrible danger. For an instant he seemed to see his wife furiously accusing him: 'Is this how you look after us?' Jamie hauled the Jaguar hard to the south and prayed he would have time to eject before *Lightning* ploughed into the meadows along the river.

Cathy thought she was dreaming. Out of the black sky an aircraft swooped into the close. As it curled round, its nose dropping, she saw it was a Jaguar and that it was below the height of the tower. One of its engines was flaring. She opened her mouth to scream.

12

TWO

Alan probed the darkness with his torch. His other hand held a household candle and a box of matches to light it with. He was several steps down into the chapel of Rycharde's shrine when a sudden and extraordinary sound drowned out even the booming of the midnight bell high in the tower. It was as if an express train were approaching. It made no sense. At the top of the stairs, about to follow him, Lucy, too, was puzzled and held the heavy door open as she peered into the darkness for some clue.

Something smashed through the huge round tower of stained glass high in the west side of the tower. Lucy thought it must be a fiery angel or a bomb. As the whole building shook at the impact and the express-train sound climaxed in an explosion so loud she thought her eardrums would burst, she instinctively swung the heavy wooden and iron door shut to protect her brother and dived for shelter behind the nearest monument. It was the last thing she remembered before everything went black.

As the well-oiled lock engaged and held, streams of fire flared through the nave as the

13

Jaguar's fuel tanks severed. Splintered glass slashed dangerously through the air and heavy crushing stone crashed, smashed and bounced crazily. The Jaguar pitched madly beneath the roof and careered sideways towards the top of the massive stone screen that separated the nave from the choirstalls. The midnight bell sounded chaotic as all the others rolled and swung. The Jaguar smashed into the top of the screen and ricocheted up to the roof. As the splintering screen spat stone, two columns in the nave which had held firm for eight hundred years crumbled like sand and the tower above began to break up and collapse. The impact shattered Lucy's protecting monument and spun her into the exploding air like a rag doll. The tall spire shivered, rocked, steadied, rocked. And fell.

Alan knew none of this. All he knew was that Lucy had suddenly slammed the heavy door shut and some sort of earthquake had happened. He lay on his side curled up in a corner of the chapel containing St Rycharde's shrine and moaning as the deep shaking and roaring rocked and jolted him. He did not know how long it had been since he had been hurled by some strange force down the sharp painful steps and had rolled himself instinctively into a tight ball waiting for the nightmare to end. It could have been thirty seconds or thirty minutes before the floor and walls stopped moving.

Alan cautiously unwound and sat up. In the pitch black he could see nothing. He had lost his right trainer and his jeans were torn. Both knees hurt and felt sticky. He was coughing a lot in the thick air and guessed that it must be full of dust so he pulled out his hanky and used it as a face mask while his scared breathing settled down. Although he ached and had a sharp pain in his knees, he could move his limbs. He knew his voice and hearing were working: the coughing proved that. His greatest fear was that he might be blind and his breathing suddenly rasped and jumped in panic. This could not be real. He must be dreaming. Yet he knew he was not and his breathing laboured even more desperately. Alan forced himself to relax – and think.

What had happened? Lucy had slammed the door to the shrine shut and he had fallen – or been thrown – down the steps. Then there had been the terrifying movement of walls and paving stones beneath his feet. And the noises. Why had Lucy wanted to imprison him? Where was Lucy? Was she safe? What had happened to her? Was she hurt? Was she scared? The thoughts were too difficult and Alan cleared his mind as best he could. There were questions that were easier to answer.

There must have been some sort of explosion or earthquake. He was in the chapel with Rycharde's shrine and only Lucy knew it. If Lucy were all right she would be able to direct the searchers to him. He was sure there would be searchers; whenever buildings collapsed – if that was what had happened – there were always rescue services immediately on the scene. He had seen it on television a hundred times; the close would be a hectic place now. But what if Lucy could not tell the rescuers where he was?

He forced himself to keep calm. When his mother discovered that Lucy and he were not at Broomyard or at home and that her cathedral keys were gone she would put two and two together. The search would begin and they would eventually come to the crypt. At the thought of his mother Alan suddenly found himself sobbing and tried to pull himself together.

Were there things he should be doing? How could he help people to find him?

The first thing was to see if he could get out of the chapel. The room was small – about seven metres by four – and the only thing it contained was the tombstone of Rycharde of Archenford. He decided to explore while he waited for rescue. He might even find his trainer. And somewhere down with him in the darkness was his torch; he might find the matches and candle. He coughed several times as dust hit the back of his throat again. What corner was he in? He had no idea. He set out to find the steps he had been hurled down.

Very carefully he got to his feet, surprised to find that his balance was very unsteady in the darkness, then, very slowly, he began to feel his way clockwise round the crypt. The moment he located the stairs or the tomb he would know where he was. After that he would begin examining the floor for his trainer, torch and matches.

For the first time he noticed that total silence had replaced the terrifying din and shouted a few times. Encouraged, he experimentally called out to his sister. 'Lucy? ... Lucy?' His voice sounded dull and small in the stone chapel. It did not even sound like his voice. 'Lucy? Lucy? Lucy?' To his dismay Alan found he could not stop. His voice became shrill with anxiety and at last the dust caught him by the throat and broke up his frantic calling in the spasm of coughing.

Alan felt sick and needed to sit down. He sank unsteadily to the ground but found himself rocking wildly on some sort of ledge and immediately hauled himself to his feet again, alarmed. He felt around the object. It seemed to be of metal and wood. He could feel splintered and torn wooden slivers and it slowly dawned that he was touching the heavy door that Lucy had closed on him. He sat down carefully and laid the handkerchief across his mouth to keep out the thick air. If the door had been forced down into the crypt, what was blocking his way out?

He began searching even harder for the steps, suddenly aware that perhaps all he had to do was climb them to be back in the cathedral near the treasury. Escape could be that close.

He forced himself to be methodical and began to half walk, half crawl to a wall – any wall. From there he began to make his way clockwise round the edges of the crypt and, on his second wall, collided painfully with the steps and damaged one of his sensitive kneecaps. Although

Alan was hurt he had other matters on his mind. At last he knew whereabouts in the chapel he was.

Alan made his way to the bottom of the twelve steps and carefully climbed. He had to move with care; they were covered with rubble and dust. When he got to the ninth step he found he could go no further and his mind told him the blank bad news that what his hands could feel was solid stone. He accepted with a dull despair that whatever had happened had collapsed a part of the cathedral and that the collapse was now blocking the only way out of the Shrine Chapel. He listened intently but all was quiet.

Alan sat thoughtfully. There should be ambulances, fire-engines, police – a lot of noise. He could hear nothing. It was a sign of how thoroughly the crypt was sealed off. Alan felt sick and threw up, time after time. When at last his stomach was empty he leaned back against the intrusion of stone and shut his eyes, gathering strength to search for his torch and trainer.

He longed for Lucy. 'Lucy, where are you?' he moaned.

'Just had an absolutely incredible report from the newsroom,' said the presenter of the all-night music show on the local radio station. 'The cathedral at Archenford's been struck by a missile. No casualties reported as yet but the cathedral's badly damaged. Unbelievable. We'll keep you informed.' He switched on the next music track and grinned through the glass to his

18

producer. 'You're having me on, aren't you? It's a wind-up, isn't it?'

The twenty-third 999 call came through to the Archenford police switchboard. Like all the others, it reported an explosion in the middle of town.

Silent and pale, Sara and Cathy sipped mugs of coffee in Sara's front room. 'The police and everybody know I'm here, don't they?' Cathy asked.

Sara reassured her. 'Anyway, they'll be letting you back into the close very soon.'

Cathy hoped so. 'If you could just have *seen* it, Sara,' she said.

'Nightmare,' agreed her friend. 'Thank goodness Lucy and Alan are well out of it at Broomyard.'

Cathy nodded and held out her hand; it was still shaking.

THREE

Lucy was slowly gathering her senses. She lay quite still, unable for several minutes to risk moving her body or even opening her eyes. As her brain began to work she remembered fragments of a nightmare. She had been dreaming she was somewhere in the cathedral. Then something had happened. Her brain would not tell her what it was. Her back told her, however, that she was pressed painfully against something that dug into her. She began easing herself away but gasped at the many sharp pains that twisted and hurt her.

She could barely move. She seemed to be more or less sitting up and leaning back. Gently raising her left arm she investigated the tight space. Her head was resting on a stone. She cautiously raised her head and felt the vivid shock of seeing nothing. She swivelled her eyes, causing her head to throb, and was immediately more careful. She thought she could make out a slight smudge of light near her feet but could not be sure. Then her head rapped against a hard surface and she made herself relax as well as she could.

The silence began to impress itself. It was strange; she had never thought that there might be different sorts of silence but what she was hearing now was not at all like the silence of, say, the night camping in the countryside with Dad and Alan. She began to identify what made it different: the sounds of her own breathing and groaning were loud, magnified, and they were the only sounds she could hear. There was another difference. She was finding it more difficult to breathe than she ever had. It was not like asthma or being out of breath after swimming. It was – well – stranger than that. Lucy felt sick and dizzy but guessed that was a result of the shock . . . of what? A sudden image flashed across her mind: a . . . something . . . smashing through the high rose window in the tower like a flaming . . . what?

Before she could think about it any more, the image had vanished and her brain was refusing to return it. She knew she must have had an accident. In the cathedral? What had she been doing in the cathedral?

Slowly she began to take control of herself. Whatever had happened to her, she must now do something about it. Her legs were aching and they too felt strange. Everything was strange. Her legs were drawn up but when Lucy started to ease them flat the pain made her wince and the strange thick air magnified her sharp intake of breath. She suddenly felt very hot. She made another attempt to straighten her legs.

This time something even more peculiar made no sense. Her legs were bent because there was a strange shape behind her knees. Her probing fingers found a smooth surface – very smooth. And round, like a cannon-ball. There was a pipe of some sort joining it . . . to something above her head. It was this pipe that had dug into her back and she squeezed round to use it to lever herself into another position, hoping it would not hurt.

Lucy tried to ease herself away from the unfamiliar shape. She was finding it harder to breathe and fought against panic. She was able to slide down a little – then a little more. She slipped down another few centimetres and stretched out a questing hand into the darkness round her feet and her fingertips touched a surface almost immediately. She felt around some more. The fingertips found the same surface: warm to the touch and quite smooth. It was metal. Could it be metal? She did her best to look down at the dim smudge of light and carefully explored the ground beneath her. She felt sharp stones and winced as an edge sliced into her thumb. At one spot she could feel flat smooth surfaces and guessed they were tiles. Her brain began at once to race. Tiles. Where were there tiles? Several situations suggested themselves but none made much sense. If only she could remember where she and Alan had been.

Alan. Her breath snagged in panic. Where was Alan? The invisible video in her mind clicked into playback and she had a sudden image of her brother walking down steps. Then something had smashed through the tower. The memory of Alan alarmed her and she automatically tried to clamber to her feet.

Lucy's head cracked against something very hard the moment she tried to straighten up and she cried out in pain, sinking back to her knees. Her hands went up to her head and felt warm stickiness but she couldn't tell if the blood was from her head or her thumb. Her brain was beginning to operate at last. She forced a hand carefully above her head. The object which had stunned her was a huge ring of metal and it was joined to the pipe behind her knees which connected to the cannon-ball at her feet. It made no sense. And Alan? Where was he?

Lucy's personal video suddenly played her fragments of the scene again. Her brother was walking down steps then something smashed the window. Something on fire. More fragments were coming back and making sense. Yes. The stairs down into the Shrine Chapel. Alan was shining his torch as he went down and the bells in the tower were chiming midnight . . . the bells in the tower. The tower almost directly above the door down to the treasury and the shrine.

The video turned itself off and for several seconds Lucy lay like stone, herself. Then with great delicacy she explored her surroundings once again – this time holding a shape and design in mind. Her fingers touched the rubble beneath her. They stroked the cannon-ball and followed the pipe up to the big ring no more than fifteen centimetres above her head. With growing despair she felt the smooth rounded surface all round her. There was a proof she might make and she reached carefully down to scrabble for a

e or fragment of tile. Fearful of what
prove, Lucy took a breath and struck
at the surface before her.

it gave a dull metallic clank and Lucy tried not
to scream. She knew where she was now – and
why the air was heavy and why the only suggestion of light she could see – and it was hardly
even that – was a line near her feet – and what
the cannon-ball was and why it was connected
by a thick metal rod to the top. Worst of all she
knew why the object that enclosed her was
roomier at the bottom than at the top.

The video suddenly decided to rewind and
play and Lucy remembered everything. She
unlocked the crypt door and Alan walked down
into the darkness, switching on his torch. There
had been the noise like an express train approaching and suddenly a fiery angel or demon had
shattered the rose window and, seeing the tower
shiver and fall, she had slammed the heavy door
shut to protect her brother. She remembered
diving behind a monument as the cathedral tower
fell. She even remembered being thrown through
the air. She recalled how the noise of the impact
had drowned even the tolling of the midnight
bell – and how even that noise had been briefly
covered by the combined chaos of ringing as the
bell-tower must have collapsed.

Lucy had often been in the ringing chamber
and knew the size of the bells. Face to face with
the truth she lost control. Lucy screamed and
kept on screaming. She twisted and writhed
against the clapper, giving herself up to panic.

Lucy felt her body would burst with the black terror surging up inside her. Hopelessly squealing she beat with her fists against the scary smoothness of the iron until, at last, her energy ran out. Only one bell was large enough – she was trapped in the Black Sergeant.

The chief fire officer made his report. 'Two pinnacles from the tower are down,' he said into his radio mike. 'No exterior sign so I assume they've collapsed inside.' He pushed down the speak button of his circuit radio and asked for the searchlight to sweep east of the tower. 'The roof's down,' he reported, 'and there's fire burning inside.' He told the operator of the crane to take him higher and, as the cherry-picker raised him high above the close, he spoke to his assistant at his side. 'Bad. Very bad, John. The rest of the tower's not going to hold up much longer.' They watched two more fire-engines moving into position, one with a huge floodlight.

'Good job it happened when it did,' the assistant said. 'At least the place was empty.' The crane shook slightly as it came to a halt and they raised their binoculars and scanned the building.

'Dangerous,' muttered the chief. His radio crackled into life and told him the RAF rescue team had arrived. 'What chance for the pilot, John?' the chief asked as they descended.

'No chance,' he replied bluntly. 'Not if he's still in his aircraft.'

FOUR

Alan felt his way carefully along the floor of the stone chamber, trying hard not to think of the tons of stone which might be pressing down on the crypt.

There were new sounds. The walls and ceiling seemed to be cracking distantly, as if in the chapel or chamber next door – though Alan knew well enough that there was no such place. Mostly he tried not to think of spiders; he had always been afraid of them. Alan squealed as his fingertips brushed a soft something that was not stone. He whipped his arm away and trembled in the darkness, half expecting to be aware of the slow quiet shifting of dirt and dust near his knees as the unseen horror crawled . . . where? Instead there were more distant groanings and crackings. Hardly daring to breathe he swept his fingers over the dangerous area and twenty seconds later was tying the lace of his missing trainer.

The horoscope in the local paper had said something like that. He remembered glancing through it with Michael Penn. How long ago had that been? It seemed years. The horoscope had warned that an argument with someone could bring trouble crashing down. Alan smiled grimly. There had been rows all day – and look what had happened. He could recall the rest exactly. 'Be brave. You are not helpless and must trust your Aquarian independence to get you out of your tight spot.'

Alan had covered three other sections of the floor when a new sound hit the stillness. Dirt, sand, dust. It was trickling down, somewhere in the darkness. Now it was streaming. What was going on?

Another eerie sound halted Alan in his tracks. It sounded like thin whistling very far away. The weird sound grew clearer and louder. It seemed to come from the walls and now it was piercing. Alan lay in the rubble, covering his ears, but just as his breathing began to stagger and gasp in fright there was silence.

A new sound began all round him. Alan decided to retreat to the safer angle between steps and wall but before he could move, from his left, his right, from above him and beneath his feet the menacing crackings suddenly seemed to explode. On hands and knees he scrambled towards the steps. Tiny stones were firing through the air like bullets from the splintering walls. Fragments flicked and stung him from all directions. Some caught him sharply on his face; others on his neck and the back of his hands. He shouted in pain and tried to ward the missiles off in the dark, protecting his eyes, but there were too many stones and he quickly curled into a ball. Immediately there was silence.

Alan tried to decide in which direction he would find safety in the angle between steps and wall but, as he cautiously knelt, he shouted in shock. His left knee had rolled on a small cylinder throwing him off balance and landing him on his side among the rubble. Somewhere in that impenetrable darkness, a powerful cracking split the air and a cloud of choking dust enveloped him.

Alan felt desperately all round him for the torch that had pitched him over. With the torch safely in his fist, he threw himself against the wall and as he curled up again, the ceiling fell. Alan screamed. He thought he was going to die.

The phone rang in Toby Whitmarsh's bedroom and he sleepily reached for the receiver. 'Whitmarsh,' he murmured. At his side, his wife stirred and woke.

'Who is it?' she asked drowsily. But her husband had snapped down the phone and was already out of bed. His wife put on the light, alarmed. 'What's the matter?'

Toby put on the bathroom light and ran water. 'Emergency at the cathedral,' he called. 'They need the plans.' Toby was the cathedral architect. He splashed water over his face. 'They're sending a police car for me in five minutes.'

Sara reached out and turned down the volume. The local radio updates were saying nothing new. 'What about Alan and Lucy?' she asked. 'They could be listening to this too. Shouldn't you let them know you're all right?' The phone rang and Sara left to answer it.

Cathy longed for a cigarette. 'They'll be asleep now,' she called after her friend. 'No point in worrying them or getting them excited. I'll leave it until the morning.' She wished Sara smoked.

Sara came back into the room with a strange look on her face. 'It's the station commander from RAF Meeston,' she said. 'He wants to speak to you.'

The first pair of the RAF team walked clumsily into the cathedral nave, hampered by their heavy protective gear, and joined four firemen, already laying hoses. Flames flowed down the tower pillars from the wreckage above it. The airmen reported calmly over their radios that they could see the crash site but that spilt fuel was still burning and nobody would be able to reach it for some time.

The squadron leader in command acknowledged their report and was passing it to the chief fire officer when a sudden tearing sound drew everybody's attention. The searchlights swept the building and locked on the tower. One of the remaining pinnacles swayed and toppled.

'Get out of there,' the squadron leader yelled into his radio. 'The tower's coming down. Everybody. Get out now.'

A thick crowd of onlookers jammed Broad Street and Church Street. They screamed as the immense square tower crumbled and collapsed.

FIVE

Lucy didn't know for how much longer she could stay calm. Enclosed within the stern iron Black Sergeant she could do nothing, not even move with any ease. She tried to breathe gently, knowing that the air inside the bell was becoming steadily thicker. She was grateful for the edge of light hemming the rim at her feet. She would soon have to try to get her mouth down to make the most of whatever fresh air may be available but had no idea how she could manage this.

The worst part was not knowing. Not knowing where Alan was – or even if he were alive; not knowing if there were rescuers; not knowing if her mother had discovered she and Alan were missing yet; not knowing if she should waste precious air and energy by shouting out and, in any case, not knowing how much of her shouting would be heard from underneath the Black Sergeant.

Lucy choked back her growing panic and forced herself to stay calm. She concentrated her thoughts on Alan, hoping he would be safe in the underground chapel. She whispered his name and it gave her some strange comfort. She whispered it again and had the clear sense that he was safe. Just then the bell was struck by the same enormous force that was cracking the Shrine Chapel ceiling. It sheered a slim stone column, brought down the arch it carried and then the ceiling it supported. Lucy screamed as she felt herself turned head over heels as the Black Sergeant rolled.

Alan finally dared move. He was cowering under a covering of stone and his nose was clogged with dust. He spat his mouth clear and breathed experimentally. It was bad. The air really was thick. He brushed and knocked away the rubble, then slowly uncurled on to his back and cautiously sat up. He ached and there were new discomforts to add to his torn knees but at least he was in one piece and able to move. His biggest fear had been that he might be disabled in some way and he had needed to fight his overactive imagination.

Alan hauled himself into a sitting position against the wall and coughed his lungs clean, wiping his itching nose with his sleeve which was so dusty that he sneezed violently several times. He listened intently. There was nothing to be heard now, apart from his own rasping breath.

Alan felt safer. Whatever had happened had obviously finished. He had been gripping the torch so tightly that it was hard to encourage his fingers to let it go now the immediate danger was over. Taking enormous care not to drop it he felt for the switch, praying that the battery would have strength and that the bulb was still intact.

After so much darkness the effect was dazzling and Alan blinked as the shaft of light sliced across the crypt, even though the beam was thick with dust. It was impossible to see more than a metre. He turned the beam upon the floor at his feet and was able to make out details. Breathing as cautiously as he could, Alan climbed painfully to his feet and, with the help of the torch, began an exploration of the crypt. He moved quickly, knowing that he must save the battery.

The ceiling had – as he'd guessed – fallen in. As far as he could tell, about half had collapsed though the rest had held up and to this he owed his life. Alan switched off the torch and sank on to the bottom stone step. There was no way out by the steps; the doorway was blocked by huge stones and tightly packed rubble, which extended halfway down the flight. There was no way out through the collapsed roof either. He could not escape by climbing up.

Alan got to his feet and switched on the beam again. He shuffled through the stone and slate to Rycharde's shrine. The stone canopy above the tomb was in one piece but the effigy of Rycharde which had stayed in one piece since 1370, defying the hammers of Henry VIII's vandals and Cromwell's Roundheads as well as two world wars, lay shattered in four sections among the debris on the floor. The stone platform on which the statue had lain was cracked and split open.

Alan knew how medieval people buried a

bishop or saint. The coffined body was lowered into a deep grave and a monument was placed over it at ground level. Often a statue of the saint was laid on top of the monument and became a shrine for pilgrims to visit.

Alan turned off the light again. He wished there were some other way – any other way – but his logic clearly spelled it out for him. He couldn't go up; he couldn't stay where he was. He had to go down.

Alan's instincts once more turned him away from the dreadful idea, but he could almost hear his twin sister sarcastically asking him what alternative he proposed and reminding him that (a) the rest of the ceiling could fall at any moment and (b) the air in the chapel would eventually become exhausted and he would die anyway.

Alan unwillingly shone the torch into the depths below the shattered tomb. It looked as though he would be able to climb down a couple of metres at least. After that . . . he couldn't tell. Alan trusted to luck and Rycharde. Securing the torch carefully in his anorak he stepped over the shattered monument and began feeling for a foothold as he squeezed into the unknown.

He had no idea what he would find in the pitch black below. He only knew that he was climbing down a tight shaft which had been made by men; he could see chisel marks on the stone blocks in the brief moments he allowed himself to use the torch. His toe found a jutting stone and tested it to see if it would support his weight, then, holding on firmly with his right hand, he lowered himself.

The narrowness of the shaft meant that Alan could not see what was beneath him – in any case there was not even enough space to pull the torch from his pocket. He tried not to think what would happen to him if there were another collapse or rearrangement. Alan searched the stones above his head for a handhold but without luck. His chest began to expand as his breathing turned to panic. He had the uncomfortable and frightening experience of being unable to take in all the breath his struggling lungs were calling for. He tried to make himself relax. He even tried to think of . . . well, anything – except Alan Graham jammed helplessly in a narrow stone shaft below the shattered underground chapel of a bombed cathedral.

He forced himself to think of Lucy and was astounded to have a strong feeling that she was thinking of him. His breathing reared and bucked less often and finally became level again. He believed she was alive but where? How could he reach her if she was trapped too?

At that moment his secure toehold broke from the wall and he felt himself slide and slip painfully about a metre. He came to a halt in a strange situation. His legs were dangling in mid-air and all his weight seemed concentrated around his chest. It was hard to breathe and he frantically tried to relieve the pressure by seeking a hold for his fingers and levering his weight from the scary embrace of rock and clay. Breathing was getting more and more difficult again and he kicked out with his legs. He felt himself slide down another centimetre or so. He kicked again and seemed to descend another few centimetres. He drew in his stomach and forced the breath from his lungs, kicking madly, and fell through two metres of air, landing on the rotten lid of a long wooden box which disintegrated under his weight.

Alan lay winded and dazed for several seconds as his senses returned. He fumbled for the torch and switched it on. He swung it to his left and nearly fainted to find himself staring at the grinning skull of Rycharde of Archenford, fifteen centimetres away.

'Poor old Rycharde,' murmured the head verger. 'What a disaster to happen on his feast-day.' The three vergers stood miserably in a corner of the cloisters. Their families, like all the other inhabitants of the close, had been moved out. These three waited where they could be called if they were needed.

At 1.30 a.m. the emergency committee held its first meeting. The dean had just arrived back from Oxford and could hardly take his eyes off the stricken cathedral, whereas Toby Whitmarsh could hardly bear to look. The RAF Meeston wing commander brought orders from the Ministry of Defence that there was to be no announcement of the RAF involvement for the time being. Each man laid down his priorities. The chief fire officer wanted no risks taken until they had a good assessment of the situation. The Assistant Chief Constable agreed.

The first television crew arrived and demanded permission to shoot the story from inside the close. Police Sergeant Briggs took great pleasure in refusing.

SIX

A sudden hail of small stones clattered against the Black Sergeant but Lucy continued her task with determination. She was used by now to the sudden dull clangs as chunks of masonry fell on the outside of the bell. The Black Sergeant gave good protection and at least she had more air and could even see the dim ridged interior of the heavy metal. The Black Sergeant had come to rest half-buried, on its side, but with a narrow gap through which Lucy thought she could eventually escape if she could somehow enlarge it. It seemed a long time since she had begun to prize away the smaller stones and rock the large ones loose.

Unseen debris fell nearby and she automatically pressed back from the open end. Dust billowed under the rim of the bell and she protected her nose and mouth. The moment things were quiet again she edged forward and returned to her work. Lucy was trying to loosen a jagged stone block and thought that, if she could remove it, there would be just space enough to squeeze through. The heat seemed more oppressive and she was sweating heavily

37

now, her mask of white dust streaked where the perspiration had run, but she did not dare stop. She could see lurid reflections around the dark metal rim. She knew that whatever was on fire must burn itself out sooner or later – the cathedral, after all, was mostly made of stone. But what if the bell were somehow engulfed in flame? Lucy shuddered but did not panic. She kept rocking the splintered stone.

Every now and then Lucy called out, 'Help! Alan? Hello?' She badly needed to think of Alan, her mother and her father. She knew that unless she got out she might never see them again. She called once more and heard her voice reverberate dully round the inside of the bell. Was it loud enough for rescuers to hear?

The small stone she was tormenting rocked and began to yield like a rotten tooth. Lucy shifted her body and crammed as close to the stone as she could, trying to lever it from its setting. A small stream of sand and mortar fell and at last, yelling in triumph, Lucy hauled hard and the stone rolled inside the bell with her. When the dust had cleared, Lucy took her shielding hands from her face and twisted to see what progress had been made. Her heart sank. Another stone had fallen and was plugging the space. Numbly she crawled to test its firmness; it didn't move.

Lucy refused to allow herself the luxury of tears or anger. With her teeth she picked the worst of the stone fragments from her broken fingernails and prepared to begin again. At least the hole was a bit larger and she warily wriggled her hand through and waved, enjoying the freedom. She stretched to touch the unseen debris on the outside but it seemed the depressingly familiar mixture of sharp, shattered stones and clogging dirt.

Suddenly her sore fingers stroked a different surface. It was smoother, though unpolished. It must be wood. She gingerly felt along an edge, wondering what it had been and where it had come from. Something sharp pricked her and her hand jerked back. Curious, she explored again and her excitement grew. It was a nail, and a long one at that, held by the wood but not firmly.

Five minutes later the massive nail was inside the bell and speeding her progress as it dug and picked its way round the wall of stone that was holding Lucy inside her metal tomb. A stone the size of a cricket ball came loose and Lucy threw it to the closed end of the bell with the rest. It was a small victory but at the present rate of progress she reckoned she would be able to crawl out in less than an hour. But would she be going into flames?

Alan backed away, unable to take his eyes off the skeleton spilling from the splintered coffin. He started as his back touched the rough-hewn wall of the vault. He realised he had been holding his breath for a very long time and released it in scared gasps and snatches. Still he could not break his glance from the sight – two metres away –

that no man had seen since the day the dead body of the Bishop of Archenford had been lowered to its resting-place in 1370. He was horrified. He couldn't save his torch battery – he had to have light . . .

Still shaking, he explored the rough-hewn cave room, ready for the next horror. There was nothing else in the narrow space around the coffin. The beam found a door, low in the wall, cracked and decayed, and he hurried to it. There seemed to be no handle. Anxious to leave Rycharde's coffin, Alan cautiously stretched out a hand and pushed. The door juddered a few centimetres but did not open. His fingernails were short from biting and his fingertips sore from scrabbling in the stony debris. Alan tried to force them round the top edge but could find no fingerhold. In the end he kicked at the door with the heel of his trainer.

With a surprisingly loud cracking and wrenching sound, the panel disintegrated almost at once, leaving a gap through which Alan knew he could easily clamber. He knelt on his torn knees and crawled through the small, low door. Now I know how the cat feels about the cat-flap, he thought; he almost smiled.

On the other side, Alan began clumsily to draw himself up but hit his head on a low ceiling and crouched immediately. He was in a very small corridor, about a metre wide and a metre high. He rubbed his ringing head and swung the torch beam. To his left, the corridor ended after a couple of metres, blocked by square stones as if the builders had suddenly decided to give up. On his right, however, a tiny shaft continued and angled out of sight. Forced to crawl, Alan began the uncomfortable journey.

The new section of the corridor was identical to the one he had just left. Ahead, the passage ended, blocked by rough stone, and he could see another small door, low in the wall. Alan dragged himself over and examined it. It was more strongly made than the other and crisscrossed with iron bindings. Alan groaned but when he pressed against the door, it opened easily – at first. Then he felt the bottom of the door grate against an obstruction and it jammed.

Alan kicked out with both feet. The door moved. He kicked again. It moved again. He kicked a third time, grunting with the effort, and shone the torch. There was enough of a gap. Alan snapped off the torch and put it in his pocket. Impatiently, he squeezed his way through the hatch and crouched, feeling a definite current of moving air and smelling damp earth. He sat back on his heels and reached above his head. Nothing – he could stand at last. Alan stiffly hauled himself upright and allowed himself the luxury of a stretch. He drew the torch from his pocket and switched it on.

Alan screamed. He was in a cellar of death.

The underground cave Alan found himself in had been roughly hewn from rock, though at some time part of the walls had collapsed, leaving scars of glistening red clay which gave off the sharp aromatic mustiness he had immediately noticed. Shelves of wood must have covered much of the walls but most had rotted centuries ago. Deep ledges were carved into the cave. Carefully stacked, on ledges and shelves, were the collected bones of the monks who had peopled the cathedral in its monastic days before Henry VIII had expelled them. Alan was in the charnel house.

His mouth froze in disgust as he played the beam over the round skulls, neatly gathered like so many grey footballs, three deep. Where the wooden shelves had decayed, skulls littered the clay floor, adding to the profusion of bones covering most of the ground. There were still places where the bones were neatly piled according to their identity – ribs, limbs, small delicate bones which must have been hands and feet. Alan was gaping at the human remains of generations of Archenford monks. He felt his stomach suddenly heave and was violently sick again.

Alan dropped to his knees and pushed himself hastily back to the low passage on the other side of the door. He sat, trembling. The torch beam seemed weaker and Alan reluctantly switched it off. He felt he might spend the rest of his life helplessly roaming the dark below the cathedral. How long could anybody live without water and food? A week? Less? Alan gave himself up to despair and howled. Tears washed tracks through the grime and dust on his face and his nose streamed like a baby's. How much more could he take?

*

Cathy stared into the fire. She felt numb. Lost. 'My fault, Sara. I shouldn't have kept on at Jamie, these last days.' Sara said nothing. 'Now it's too late.'

Her friend laid a comforting arm round her. 'Come on,' she said softly. 'There's still hope. You heard what the wing commander said. Jamie could have ejected. They don't know. They can't get close enough to find out.'

Cathy shook her head.

'Look,' said Sara firmly. 'I'm going to ring Tom.' Tom was their doctor.

Cathy shook her head.

'And I still think you should ring the Vaughans and tell your kids,' Sara insisted. 'You need them with you.'

At two o'clock, the chief fire officer made a brief statement to newspaper, radio and television reporters and asked for questions.

'BBC, sir. Can you tell us the situation?'

'We've pulled everybody out for the time being. The building's not structurally safe. I'm waiting for heavy lifting equipment.'

'Local independent news. Any casualties?'

'The cathedral was empty.'

'Sir? *News at Ten*. What about the reports of a low-flying aircraft and a possible collision?'

'What reports?'

'People are saying there was a low-flying air-craft in trouble. There's a rumour that eye-witnesses actually saw a plane hit the building.'

'I've heard reports the cathedral was hit by a

bomb, a missile, lightning, a plane and God knows what. When I know exactly what happened I'll tell you. That's it, gentlemen.'

'Why is the RAF here?'

'Thank you, gentlemen. I said that's it.'

'When will you give another statement, sir?'

'Every hour on the hour.'

SEVEN

Lucy too had given up. She lay curled inside the Black Sergeant too tired and dispirited to move. The more stone and rubble she managed to shift, the more seemed ready to drop and take its place. Since the most recent fall, there was less of a gap than there had been an hour earlier. Now there was hardly enough to squeeze her arm through and she had long ago lost the energy to keep up her regular shouting. The strangest thing was that she was losing interest. Her situation no longer had the terror and unreality of a nightmare. It was almost as if she were bored.

Lucy tried to think of her mother and father but was not surprised to find that the images no sooner appeared in her mind than they started to break up. She coughed painfully and shifted her position to the best she could find in the bell. Thoughts of Alan stayed longer but filled her with hopelessness. She instinctively knew that somewhere in the ruins of the cathedral her brother was despairing too. Her eyes and nose were streaming now but as she reached with difficulty for the filthy, ragged handkerchief jammed in her jeans pocket, her tender fingers stung and she gave up.

45

Lucy leaned back against the slightly warm curvature of the bell and did her best to concentrate on Alan. In spite of her wild sobbing, she needed to send him a message. 'Don't give up. Don't dare give up.' The words hung in her mind like a lantern for a moment before they started to dim and disintegrate. She fought to reassemble them and angrily wiped her eyes with her torn sleeve. She must not give way like this.

'Stop it!' she shouted, hearing her voice break and echo around the ring of iron. She was shouting for both of them now. 'Stop it, Alan! Don't give up!'

Lucy fought the tears and twisted back down to the larger end of her dark prison. She felt for the nail in the gloom, found a suitable piece of rubble and obstinately began work again.

Alan examined the charnel house carefully with his weakening torch. He was more and more worried about the dimming of the beam. It had taken a lot of will-power to force himself back into the cave of bones but he had suddenly felt that Lucy was somehow willing him on. He knew it made no sense. He guessed that it must also have something to do with the scary release of despair he had just been through. The important thing was, he felt better. He would not give up. Lucy would not let him.

But was there a way out?

He trod carefully among the carpet of bones, trying not to walk on them, and examined a corner where the ceiling had collapsed, bringing down part of the wall. Suddenly he flinched at the sight of something moving. It was a worm. Alan drew close. He watched it squirm and turn in the unaccustomed light. He lifted a gentle finger and touched it, seeing the creature wince and twist at the strange touch. Alan moved closer; it was the first living thing he had seen since Lucy had slammed the door on him and the world had gone crazy.

The worm was white and at least as thick as a pencil. Alan had never seen a worm exactly like this. It had strange markings. The light of the torch revealed two dark spots that looked remarkably like eyes which twisted and seemed to scan every detail of the boy's face. Alan was aware of more movement and drew back as another blunt face thrust itself from the glistening clay into the dim beam and – even as he gently reached to touch the new arrival – a third emerged and waved slowly before the boy's amazed glance. Alan felt mesmerised as another, and yet another, and then two at the same time, drew themselves slowly through the apparently solid wall.

Alan shook his head, puzzled. What were they reacting to? The light? His presence? Some strange signal that was passing between them? Alan glanced to his left as three new worms squirmed out and probed the air. There was another, another, another. And suddenly the wall was a writhing living surface.

As the twisting worms broke up the surface of

the wall and a definite smell of decay filled the underground cavern, Alan grew more and more disturbed. He could not pull his eyes from them as he considered the possibility that the blind squirming creatures were descendants of those worms that had cleaned the flesh from the bones piled all around and that it was the presence of human meat that was calling them now. Alan stepped further back as a hundred pairs of eyes blindly swung this way and that, as if seeking their newest prey.

Alan spat and snapped off the beam. He forced himself to stand silently in the dark, telling himself that the worms were creatures of the clay and would not leave it. He counted thirty and switched the light on again. The wall was empty. Alan stared – but the weak beam flickered and he pulled himself together. He turned from the clay wall and forced himself to move deeper into the bone-house.

There was a section he had not felt able to examine because it was deep in the remains of the long-dead monks. He took a breath and approached it now.

Most of the shelving still clung to the wall though at one spot the black wet wood had fallen apart and collapsed. In several places it sagged under its load and looked as if the slightest disturbance would bring even more bones tumbling down. Alan was shining the beam into the heap of skulls, searching for a low hatch, like the others, when the beam flickered and went out. His heart jumped. He shook the torch hard and shouted in relief when it came on again. Then he saw the corner of a low door behind a high pile of bones. He crouched and studied how best to move it. He had known all along that sooner or later he would have to touch the bones.

Carefully Alan reached out and touched a long flat bone. It felt like wood or dusty plastic. This was a relief. He gently closed his fingers and lifted it, testing its weight. It moved easily, only slightly more heavy than a desk ruler, which it resembled. Alan felt encouraged and began working faster. Always keeping the dimming beam on the bones he began shifting and lifting with one hand, respectfully placing them to one side, unable to forget that these bones had once carried flesh, blood and brains – or that his bones could end up among them.

The thought made him work faster. He wedged the torch in the corner of a stone ledge near his shoulder and angled the beam on the section where he was working. With two hands he was able to work surprisingly quickly and the top edge of the door began to appear. Alan lifted a skull and, with his other hand, reached out to something he thought he recognised as part of a pelvis. As he paused to examine it, two thick wires curled menacingly from the eye socket of the skull and hauled a squat hairy body into his terrified sight. Alan froze. At the same moment there were movements beneath his other hand. He could not tear his glance away from the monster slowly emerging from the skull but, from the corner of his eye, he sensed several shadowy shapes scurry deeper into the heap. They were big enough to topple a clavicle which rattled as it slid to the ground.

Alan hurled the skull as far from him as he could and scrambled desperately away, hearing his voice high-pitched and squealing. His wide eyes flicked over the bones for more spiders and his panic dislodged the torch. It fell among the bones and went out.

Alan hardly dared breathe. Rattling and scraping, bones fell all round him, noisily rearranging themselves. The skull with the spider had dislodged more bones to his left. There was a bony rocking as, perhaps, a skull balanced itself. Finally, there was silence and Alan was alone with the dark once more. And with the spiders.

Now he did not panic. His fear and horror drove him into an iciness he had never known before. There was nothing more to lose. He pushed his hands through the darkness to where he remembered the outline of the top edge of the door. His fingers slid through bones which fell and, for all he knew, through thick nests of watching spiders but he did not think about it. It was impossible to feel a fear more heart-stopping than he had just encountered. Alan was locked into a cold sort of courage.

He never knew how long it took him to clear the door, open it, drag himself through and jam it shut behind him. Safe in a low passage, on the other side of the door, Alan collapsed into uncontrollable trembling, fighting the compulsion to strip off every bit of his clothing for fear that even the smallest spider might be caught in it.

As the trembling eased and the possibility of a further move returned, he was aware of two new factors. There was a faint sense of fresh air and the degree of darkness had lightened very, very slightly. He cautiously swept the floor with his hands and screamed as his fingers touched the unexpected. He scrambled away and shivered in the darkness while his disturbed brain deciphered what it was. He swiftly crawled back to find it. It had been twisted and flattened. It was cold, hard and a fragment had broken away. Nevertheless, a tapering stem and flat base identified it beyond doubt. It was a small, thin-metalled chalice and he knew where it must have come from.

The reporter from the *Express* finished dictating his three hundred words over the portable phone and told the secretary in London that the excitement seemed to be over. 'It's quiet now, dear,' he said. 'I can see a bit of burning through the windows. But that's all. The crowd's more or less thinned out too.' He signed off and wandered over to the photographer. 'Let's get back to the hotel,' he said. 'Nothing's doing here.'

The dean walked across the close to the vergers and watched with them in silence. 'Terrible,' he muttered. They nodded.

Two hundred metres away, the joint team from the RAF and the fire service were back inside the cathedral. Visibility was better; much of the smoke had been drawn outside by three giant air expellers. Grateful nevertheless for their oxygen masks, the six men moved with great care towards the south transept which, from outside, had appeared the least damaged part of the building. They were still some way from the wrecked Jaguar. They reported hearing debris and rubble fall and shift from almost all parts of the building.

Toby Whitmarsh walked to the corner of the close where lighting was being rigged to flood the cathedral's dark west end. He pulled at his gloves and gave his scarf an extra wind round his freezing neck.

A bored ITN cameraman was grateful for this new activity. As the bright sheet of light swept across the west end, he practised zooms and focuses. He zoomed in and out of the statues above the huge, magnificent doors. He zoomed in and out of the window above. He moved higher and zoomed in, focused and began recording.

Toby Whitmarsh stared at the crack spreading twenty metres up beneath the heavy pinnacles at the top of the west end and widening before his eyes. He ran, shouting to warn the council workmen setting up the floodlights directly below.

The chief fire officer sat with the station commander in the emergency headquarters caravan studying the detailed floor plans of the cathedral and listening intently to the damage reports. They looked up as the police inspector rushed in. Then they heard the noises begin.

EIGHT

A strange shivering suddenly engulfed Lucy and for a moment she was not sure whether it had come from inside her or from outside. She had felt feverish for a long time now. It must have something to do with shock. As she paused, half-crouched, painfully half kneeling in the stuffy restricted space she felt the tremors again. The ground beneath the bell trembled and the Black Sergeant rocked twice, causing the immense clapper to shift a few grinding centimetres. There were eerie crashes somewhere far away which boomed and echoed. Lucy stayed quite still. The strange movements made her feel sick and she pulled back into her prison as the Black Sergeant shifted slightly again and settled. Apart from a fall of light debris on the outside which lasted several seconds, there was nothing else.

Lucy opened her eyes, screwing them up against the everlasting dust, relieved to discover that nothing seemed to have changed for the worse. If anything, the dim light was a little stronger and she eased the weight from her aching legs and leaned forward to begin work on the diamond-shaped rock again. The tremor had helped her. The stone seemed wedged differently now. She waggled it experimentally and began digging away with her long nail. She forced in the nail deeply and levered against the packed rubble, then, when it seemed to find a deeper gap, Lucy began using the nail in a vigorous stirring motion. The nail snapped.

She desperately felt for the lower half jammed deep into the crack but could only just reach it with the tip of a finger and knew she had no chance of recovering it. She tried to rock the larger stone but it would move no further than before.

Lucy gave up. It seemed her roughness and impatience had robbed her of the best chance to escape. Lucy's eyes felt tired. The dust under the lids was building up again and she set herself to blink fast twelve times to wash the dust away. After the eighth blink she felt herself sliding into a doze and did not fight it. Lucy leaned back against the smooth wall of the giant bell, surprised to find she was not afraid. It was best to allow her body to do as it needed. She thought that perhaps it was telling her that she had done everything possible and now there was only the waiting left – which would pass more swiftly if she were asleep. She blinked twice more but somewhere before the final blink, sleep drifted comfortably over her and her painful, dust-coated body gently relaxed against her captor's iron walls. Her breathing slowed, rasping into a quiet rhythmical snore.

It was an extraordinary dream. She was feverish again, shivering violently, shaking, then falling among crashing stone through the darkness of sleep. A split second before she hit the ground she seemed to dream that she woke and found it was not, after all, a dream. But by then it was too late and she was unconscious again.

The same series of tremors sounded to Alan like distant tube trains heard from a nearby cellar. The moment the rumbling began he froze, alert, wishing he still had the torch, and when, after several seconds, it seemed to move away, he forced himself to push on with twice the urgency. Now that he knew where he was, he was determined to get to his destination before the next tremor which might be less gentle. Still unable to believe his luck, he checked yet again the shattered ceiling in the passage outside the charnel house and almost cheered at a definite suggestion of light. His eyes were very sensitive to light now. It was not daylight but had the feeling of the very early morning before dawn. Alan carefully laid down the battered chalice and fixed his grip on a thin slab of paving. He heaved it a few centimetres aside, enough to squeeze past.

The next tremor was alarming. Alan heard the distant rumbling again but this time it approached so fast that it seemed as if an underground train was about to appear any second. The closer the sound came, the more he was aware of everything around him shaking and shifting. The paving stone grated and slid another few centimetres and then there was a slow splintering sound which climaxed into a monstrous cracking and Alan felt himself painfully pushed back down the steep slope of rubble that had taken so long to climb.

As he hit the sand and stones back at the foot of the heap he curled up, shielding his face until the deafening rumbling moved away. He gingerly looked around him and was relieved to see that nothing much had changed. He remembered the head verger's gloomy statement that disasters always came in threes and scrambled as fast as he could back to the paving slab at the top of the pyramid of rubble. From there, he could get through the smashed floor of the cathedral treasury, where the chalice had come from.

The cathedral treasury was built to withstand burglary, fire and all foreseeable disasters. Ten years earlier, a security firm had installed strong steel rods to reinforce the walls and keep the priceless exhibits safe. The rods had done their job well but, although the walls were intact, the floor had collapsed in one corner. Alan was grateful for this as he hauled himself through the torn flagstones and sat, gasping for breath. All round him, chalices lay scattered beneath a cracked display case hanging uselessly from the wall.

Most of the silver and gold exhibits had survived well but the display cases had – all but one – shattered, leaving the floor a dangerous hazard of razor-sharp glass fragments. Jewelled and enamelled reliquaries, silver maces and gold plates littered the floor. The magnificent display of vestments and fabrics had been almost completely wrenched from the walls. Mappemonde, the priceless medieval map of the world, hung from its stand in tatters, sliced and shredded by flying glass.

The greatest miracle as far as Alan was concerned was that he could see. High in two of the walls, a series of small round windows, like portholes, permitted dim light to trickle in. Alan was relieved to see the pale glow which suggested that there were strong lights outside the cathedral. Rescue lights, he fervently hoped. Best of all, he knew that he was now on the way back up to ground level. The treasury was on the same level as Rycharde's shrine, where he had begun.

Alan wasted no time. In the corner was the service lift which operated between the underground room and the level above, carrying small exhibits, cleaning materials and anything else that needed to be moved. The tapestry hiding the hatch door had been half torn from the wall and was difficult to pull clear but Alan was relieved to see, after a minute's struggle, that the door behind it was gaping open. The dim light did not illuminate the shaft and, peering up inside, hoping to see where the travelling-box was, Alan was just deciding he would have to risk the climb, when, without warning, the third and most violent tremor attacked the treasury.

There was an explosion. A blinding cloud of dust swept into the air. Glass began to fly and Alan felt a searing pain along a forearm as he threw himself into the protection of the hatch.

There was one final enormous percussion. It felt as if something immense had slammed into the shaft somewhere above him. Everything shook and Alan shouted in terror until dust clogged his throat, making him choke. As soon as the shattering noise had subsided and the shaking had ceased, Alan began climbing in a new panic, determined to be as close to ground level as possible.

The lift shaft had suffered from the impact of whatever must have hit it. For the first two metres, Alan was able to find a direct way up but then his progress was blocked by a tangled network of metal. He felt blindly round the obstruction and groaned. He had guessed right. Something had crashed down into the lift shaft and was now blocking his progress. His searching fingers probed the twisted metal and jagged stone – and then touched something different. It was smooth; it was rounded; most strange of all, it was slightly warm. Puzzled, Alan jammed himself into a position where he could investigate more thoroughly. His fingers found carving. He shifted his position so he could follow the line of words round. Almost at once he knew what the surface was and what lay beneath his disbelieving fingers.

YE FOR WHOM I CALLE SHAL HEARE MEE NEVERE

Suddenly sombre, Alan let out his breath. Until this moment he had thought only of limited damage, mostly below ground. Now he knew that matters were equally bad up at ground level, and probably even higher. The massive tower was down. What other explanation could there be for this of all things – the Black Sergeant – to have fallen so far? Alan, like most people, considered the death bell bad luck and quickly began finding a way round. The new discovery made him fearful for his sister. Where was Lucy?

'Inspector? We're from ITN. Can you tell us anything?'

'You've got eyes. The west end of the building is down. Information is that the collapse has triggered further damage to other sections of the cathedral.'

'Reuters New Agency, Inspector. Any casualties? We've seen the ambulances – civil and RAF.'

'Nobody hurt outside. We had a reconnaissance team inside at the time. Minor injuries. They're out now and safe.'

'Inspector? BBC local radio news. Are you still denying the initial damage was caused by a low-flying plane hitting the cathedral?'

'We've never denied that. It's always been among the possibilities. I have to go now.'

'What about the pilot of the plane, sir?'

'I have no information.'

'Will the chief fire officer be making a further statement?'

'In an hour.'

*

'So there we are,' said the presenter of the local radio's all-night music show. 'It's a real tragedy for Archenford. We'll have a statement from the dean of the cathedral for you in half an hour and the man himself will be in the studio at six to share his feelings with us. That's the regional news at three a.m. on the morning that our finest building was hit by a plane – reported by eye-witnesses to be a Jaguar from RAF Meeston.'

Sara watched Cathy dial the Vaughan's number. Now that it was out in the open that a Meeston Jaguar was involved, it was best that Lucy and Alan should hear the story from their mother. She took the coffee mugs into the kitchen and ran hot water. The phone went down hard and Sara turned, smiling. 'That didn't take long.'

Cathy was in the door, very pale. 'They're not there,' she gasped. 'Drive me to the close. I've got to check my keys.' Sara dried her hands and hurried out after Cathy. She wondered if she should worry about Michael; no, he was always telling her he could look after himself. She hoped he was right.

NINE

Lucy could not move. Now she knew she had not been dreaming and guessed the Black Sergeant had fallen. She had no idea where it had come to rest. She knew only three things. She was in the pitch dark; she was pinned on her side by the huge immovable clapper; her back radiated pain which was all the worse because she couldn't move. For the first time since she had seen the tower window shatter, Lucy thought she might die. She struggled frantically to free herself but could hardly move and the sharp pain stopped her feeble efforts within seconds.

This was strange. Lucy tried to focus her thoughts. She supposed there were things she must do in the last moments of life. She knew she should pray – though she didn't really believe in God and wondered if her prayer would count now since it was only because she was afraid and hurt. She was amazed how calm she felt now that she had accepted she would not get out of the bell. She wondered who would find her body. It would be a shock for someone.

Lucy had heard that the whole of one's past

life played in the mind like a videotape on fast forward but there was no sign of that yet. Instead, the only images that came to her mind were of her family. Mum getting the supper earlier that night, before she went out to see Sara; it had been spaghetti with her own special sauce, their favourite. Dad yesterday at McDonald's, trying to be extra-jokey to cover up the problems. Alan's face turning to her, puzzled at the sudden strange noise filling the cathedral. The images suddenly fragmented and Lucy felt the blood drain from her face as she heard the scratching sounds. Her calmness shattered. Panic took its place.

Rats.

They had been an unspoken and unacknowledged terror, always at the back of her mind as she half imagined them, slipping deftly through the shadows of the wrecked buildings. Lucy remembered the strange night-time scrabbling sounds in the Cornwall holiday house and the hypnotising horror of finding a rat rooting about in the kitchen waste bin – the paralysing terror as it jumped past her. Those noises came clearly to her now. Scratching, scraping, scrabbling.

Lucy's mouth opened but the scream would not come. A high whimpering sound happened instead – and kept on happening.

Alan froze, heart jumping, and twisted urgently in the shaft to a more watchful position. He waited for the shock to subside and his brain to allow him to think. He listened hard. Where had the noise come from? What was it? Was it dangerous? A cat? It sounded like a cat. What else had a voice as high? He waited.

The mewing noise faded and his breathing levelled out. He listened intently one last time. There was no sound; nothing happened. He climbed on.

Alan twisted in the tight shaft and found a good climbing position. He kicked a new foot-hold, dislodging a fall of rubble which pattered against the half-buried bell now a good three metres below. He shivered as immediately the strange muffled sound came again but forced himself to pay no attention. In any case he must almost be at the top of the shaft.

Alan was wrong. It took five more minutes of careful, cramped progress before his head at last came level with the service hatch on the floor above. He hooked his grazed and aching elbows over the edge and painfully levered himself up, toppling into a corridor where he lay squinting into the gloom, panting and exhausted. From what he could see, amazingly, there seemed to be little damage done – an area of roof-fall and a door torn from its hinges. But the light was almost non-existent; he supposed his eyes must be accustomed to darkness.

At this new level he listened intently for the sound of rescue services as he rubbed his sore eyes and relaxed against the cold stone wall. It was a relief to be here. Peering into the darkness he could see that plaster had fallen from the wall in several places but he was at last nearly back at ground level. He hauled himself to his feet and stretched experimentally. He felt tired and ached all over.

Alan could not get the animal sound out of his mind. Had it really come from inside the Black Sergeant? His mind tried to imagine what it must be like to be trapped inside the bell but he forced the images away. They were too horrible. It must have been a cat; nothing else made that sort of noise.

Alan got stiffly to his feet and turned towards the shop door. He delicately touched the long burning cut on his arm and winced. His mind returned to the bell. What if it was Chloe from the deanery or Dorabella, the organist's cat? What if it was the head verger's Princess? Alan peered into the gloom. The shop door would be just round the corner. He turned his tired head back to the hatch. A major part of his intelligence told him he was about to do the most stupid thing of his life and, five minutes later, he lowered himself carefully on to the Black Sergeant and whistled softly.

Lucy was petrified; fear had turned her to stone; that was how it felt. Or ice. She jammed her hand over her mouth to stifle the whimpering as whatever horror was ranging slyly over the Black Sergeant's surface dislodged small stones and sand. She was terrified of letting the thing know where she was or how fearful. Into the terrifying stillness and silence a new sound came.

To Lucy, it sounded like long drawn-out squeaking and her aching body twitched in distress, remembering how the rat had squeaked, cornered in the kitchen, as Dad killed it with the coal shovel. Lucy moaned as the sound came again – though this time the rat-squeaking sounded a bit like Alan whistling to Chloe or Princess when they ranged through the Graham garden but Lucy knew that was impossible.

'Chloe?'

Lucy gasped and shut her eyes. This was worst of all. Perhaps none of this was real. Lucy had, for whatever reason, gone mad.

'Princess? Dorabella?'

Lucy started shouting. The words were meaningless, forced out by fear. They echoed and redoubled inside the Black Sergeant, hurting her ears, making everything worse – if it could be worse. Exhausted she finally subsided into dumb misery.

'Lucy?'

The voice was perfect, close to the open end of the bell, quiet, shaky, frightened, and brilliantly wonderful. 'Lucy? Is it you? Lucy?' Alan's voice rose.

'Alan!' Lucy was suddenly sobbing, though whether in relief or madness she couldn't tell since there didn't seem to be any difference. Alan called back to comfort her but once she had begun, the sobbing seemed to go on for a long time. Then her brother's tentative hand came probing into the bell and his fingers touched her own. That was when the sobbing stopped and neither moved or said anything for several minutes.

Cathy sat in the emergency HQ and went over the events of the early evening for the fourth time. The others made notes and consulted the plans in silence. Cathy was distraught.

'You've got to do something,' she shouted suddenly. 'Not just sit here!' Sara squeezed her hand and the chief fire officer nodded understandingly.'

'Mrs Graham,' he said gently, 'the cathedral is in a highly dangerous and unstable condition. If I order my men inside, I risk their lives. We must be certain Lucy and Alan are there, and fairly sure in which part.' Cathy shut her eyes.

The *Express* reporter was taking down background information from the vergers when the vans were waved into the close and the barking dogs led out by their handlers.

'Interesting. That must mean there's somebody still in the cathedral then,' he muttered. The doors of the HQ caravan opened and Sara and Cathy emerged with a policewoman. 'Who's that?' he asked.

The head verger followed his glance. 'Mrs Graham,' he said. 'Works for the dean.'

The reporter watched her distress as the women entered the Archdeacon's house. 'Has she got any family?' he mused.

'Twins. Boy and girl,' the head verger replied. 'Her husband's in the RAF,' the youngest verger chipped in before the others could stop him. 'A pilot.'

The reporter's eyes gleamed. 'Thanks,' he called, hurrying away.

TEN

Alan wanted to begin shifting the smaller stones as soon as his sister would let go of his hand but she would not release him because by now she was not sure of what was real and what was not.

Alan understood how his sister felt. He could see nothing of his twin as he held her hand and stroked her fingers, talking quietly and reassuringly about things that had happened yesterday or last week or last year until eventually he guessed she was ready to believe she was really and truly no longer on her own. He didn't tell her what was all round them, hidden from her sight. In fact he hardly even dared think of it himself. He waited for the right moment and gently withdrew his hand from inside the monster half-buried bell. Lucy said nothing and let him go.

Setting Lucy free was not easy. The lift shaft was narrow and there was very little room to work in. Alan began pulling away the small stones. They made little difference but he thought it would help Lucy's confidence to see the small gap quickly growing until, at last, she would be able to take a part in her own escape. She could not shift much stone herself, but she could tell Alan which stones seemed to be the important ones to shift. They worked in silence until there was a gap he thought big enough for her to wriggle through. Alan slumped back, his hands hot and torn. He called to Lucy but Lucy still could not move.

Lucy bit back tears of frustration as she fought to manoeuvre herself round the rubble and stone but there was no room for balance or leverage. The broad immovable barrier clapper was another obstruction. A third was the pain in her cramped back.

'You're not trying.' Alan was becoming exasperated and frightened. What would happen if Lucy could not be brought out? He reached into the Black Sergeant and gripped her wrist. He pulled hard but could not draw her out without much more help from inside. 'Help yourself,' he shouted angrily. 'You're not trying.'

Lucy tried another twisting manoeuvre. 'I am,' she called, squeezing round the iron shaft. Alan's hand grabbed her elbow and he hauled at Lucy's arm, knowing he must be hurting her, urging her on until finally a bleeding hand and then a bruised and grazed arm emerged and, finally, Lucy's wide eyes staring from her filthy streaked face. In the gloom, as he came very close, Alan could just make out her features and was shocked at her appearance but he forced a grin. 'All right, Lucy. Come on. We can do this. You and me together, we can get out of all this.'

*

Lucy lay in the rubble of the shop corridor at the top of the service shaft. It was the first time she had been able to assume her full length for more than two hours and her back felt less painful. Alan lay slumped beside her. For a full ten minutes they rested in silence, panting with exhaustion, until they instinctively turned to each other and hugged, clinging on hard.

It was something they had never done before. They clung to each other as they had so often seen disaster survivors on television cling in the sheer relief of finding each other alive. As they moved apart something immense crashed somewhere beneath them and they were suddenly choking in the dust that jetted in thick yellow clouds from the service shaft. Lucy guessed that the Black Sergeant's massive weight had caused yet another fall. They knew they had to move and cautiously stepped along the corridor towards what had been the cathedral shop.

They stood where the door had been and peered into the almost total darkness. A display of handmade dolls lay tossed and broken in the debris like grotesque miniature victims of some toytown disaster. Everything else was a shattered mess.

'Find candles from the shelves near the pottery,' said Lucy. 'I'll look for matches.'

Alan didn't reply. He was exploring the floor by cautiously sweeping the mess with his hands along the floor and had soon found one of the carrier bags. He knew there would be boxes of small candles in the corner behind the door and blindly felt his way there.

'Got them!' Lucy's voice was triumphant. She struck a match. Both recoiled blinking from the tiny flare of light and Alan lit a candle. It was a huge relief to have the sureness of light once again. Alan found a broken candleholder and carefully stuck the small candle in it. They felt less tired, more confident and grinned stupidly, seeing each other properly for the first time. Lucy turned. 'Let's go,' she said. Lifting the candlestick she headed for the emergency exit which would lead them to a final set of steps and up to ground level at last.

The emergency exit was useless. The handle had been sheared from the door by masonry plummeting from the roof and there was no way of operating the catch. Alan pushed hard against the heavy door but it would not budge. Lucy set down the candle and joined him. They tried desperately to shift the door but it would not move: something was jamming it fast from the other side.

'Why can't it live up to its name?' Alan shouted, kicking it angrily. 'If this isn't an emergency what the hell is?' He aimed one last hopeless kick and turned towards his sister who was already gathering up the candle.

'Come on,' she said quietly. 'It just means we've got to go through the café and kitchens.'

As they stood, watching each other's weary disappointment, a voice – so quiet they could easily have missed it – whispered, 'Alan?'

They were shocked and too scared to speak. Alan took the thin candle from Lucy and held it high. Lucy moved close to him for confidence.

'Hello?' Alan's voice was shaky and they stood in silence for several seconds before a soft groan replied from somewhere near the counter. Alan reached for his sister's hand and they shuffled forward. The dim light revealed a sprawling shape on the floor behind the counter, covered in dust and rubble.

They hurried to help. Alan knelt beside the still figure and brushed rubbish from its Balaclava helmet. He looked up helplessly as Lucy crouched at his side bringing stronger light. The figure coughed very weakly and its shoulders shivered. Brother and sister turned the figure as gently as they could.

The grey face of Michael Penn stared up at them.

There was no sign of a wound but heavy jagged fragments of roof vaulting lay close to his head. The shock and the fright redoubled.

'What are you doing here?' Lucy asked. Michael seemed not to hear her. His dull eyes stared into the darkness beyond them. His woollen helmet was torn and Lucy began carefully to draw it clear of his head but suddenly gasped. 'Oh God!' she whispered, seeing blood on her hands. The Balaclava helmet was saturated.

'Michael – can you hear me?' asked Alan. Again there was no reply but, once more, the boy began to cough and this time, although the coughing was as feeble as before, it seemed to shake his body apart. 'We ought to sit him up,' Alan whispered, more and more scared, and they set about propping his shoulders and head up. But the coughing never stopped and blood suddenly sprayed across his chest like a bib. Alan and Lucy were horrified.

'All right, Mike,' said Alan, very frightened, 'you'll be all right. You will.' The coughing faded but a terrible wheezing took its place.

'What can we do?' said Lucy desperately.

For a moment Michael focused his milky eyes and he looked from one face to the other as if puzzled to find the Graham twins there. His mouth moved. Michael clearly believed he was speaking but no words happened and this eventually puzzled him too. He looked around and his arms waved as he tried to get his balance and sit up. As Lucy and Alan supported him, Michael nodded his thanks, coughed again, slumped and they knew he was dead. Blood seeped gently from his mouth and nose. They laid him carefully on his back before getting to their feet and holding each other tight.

'It's all crazy!' Alan sobbed. 'Nothing makes sense!' Lucy stroked his hair and murmured quietly but it was a long time before they felt able to let each other go.

They looked down at Michael. They had never seen a dead body before.

'What on earth was he doing here?' Lucy asked.

Alan nodded first to the open till and then to the notes in Michael's hand. At last they knew where the money for his expensive games had come from. They stood solemnly looking down at the still figure who had played computer games at their house a few hours earlier. It was so weird that he had unknowingly shared the nightmare situation with them and they felt a surprisingly sharp sympathy for him.

Alan looked across at his sister. 'What should we do?'

Lucy shook her head. 'Nothing we *can* do,' she replied. 'Not now. Not yet. Not until we get out.'

Alan shook his head. 'No,' he said. 'There's one thing we can do.' He bent down and eased the money from Michael's fist, replaced it in the till and slammed the drawer shut. Then they covered the body with wrapping paper, found a crucifix to stand near his head and stood reverently for a while before scuffling back into the corridor. Nobody need believe Michael Penn a thief.

It took the machine and its crew twelve minutes to drill through the wall in the close at ground level. The leader of the search team sent a dog in first, then his most experienced man.

'What are they doing?' asked Cathy dully. The dean came to her from the window.

'They've knocked a way into the treasury,' he reported. 'From there, they'll drill down to the Shrine Chapel.'

The Archdeacon's wife passed Sara Penn at the phone, carrying a tray of fresh tea and biscuits.

'No luck?' she called. Sara shook her head, trying not to worry and to remember what other friends Michael might be with at the moment. She reconsidered the police inspector's suggestion that he might be with Lucy and Alan but dismissed it. She had told him that Michael wouldn't do anything so crazy but now she was having trouble convincing herself. She bit her lip and tried not to panic.

The secretary took down the dictated report and scanned the copy without emotion. She timed and dated it – 0330:16.02.94 – before sending it to the sub-editors' desk. 'Jaguar Family In Cathedral Nightmare' would be a good headline.

ELEVEN

Alan and Lucy walked in silence along the corridor to where a narrow stone staircase wound round a massive central pillar. Michael Penn's death had shocked them deeply and brought them face to face with the possibility that they might not survive. Alan wondered if the boy had suffered much pain. Lucy thought how easy it was to be in the wrong place at the wrong time. Each knew what the other must be thinking but kept the thoughts private.

Lucy led the way, holding the candle before her. For once, there was no obstruction to the circular staircase which climbed round the column and led to the cathedral café and its kitchen. Alan's nose twitched.

'Gas,' he said. They stopped. Somewhere in the deep stonewalled silence there was a distant hissing and they stood silently for another half-minute listening.

'That's not gas. It's water – I think,' said Lucy. She moved cautiously on and Alan followed.

Almost immediately she was proved right. It was the sound of water – water flowing, water splashing. Alan knelt and felt the stone step at his feet. Water slid round his fingers and down the spiral staircase.

'Of course,' he said, 'the kitchen and toilets. The pipes would be broken.'

Lucy stopped so abruptly that he almost walked into her. She turned. Alan was right too: there was a smell of gas.

'What about this flame?' she asked. They both looked doubtfully at the flickering candle.

Alan shrugged. 'I don't know,' he admitted. 'I think gas only explodes if it's compressed.' He shrugged again and they looked at each other, willing the other to take away the nagging fear. Neither wanted to give up light again.

Lucy had a sudden thought. 'Wait here.' She began to squeeze past him, returning along their route, but Alan would not let her pass.

'Where are you going? I don't want to be left in the dark on my own.'

His sister looked steadily into his eyes. 'If you were a burglar,' she said, 'what would you need to carry?'

Alan nodded slowly and lit another candle from the shoulder bag. 'Do you want me to come with you?'

Lucy knew it would be hard for her to search Michael's pockets but recognised the anxiety in his voice. 'You stay here,' she said firmly. 'I want to be able to see the light at the end of the tunnel and know it's only you.'

He watched her descend out of sight round the thick stone column, the glow of her candle growing dimmer and dimmer until it was gone and he could only hear quick shuffling steps which eventually died away too. The subterranean rumbling started up again and Alan thought he felt the steps tremble slightly. He turned and faced upward, straining ears and nose for water and gas. It was the first time he had been on his own since he had found Lucy and he hated it. The image of Michael Penn's last minutes kept flashing across his mind.

'Come on, Lucy. Come on,' he shouted suddenly. His voice echoed in the stone passageway and he had almost decided to go back down and find her when he heard steps returning and almost at once saw the flickering of her candle.

Lucy hurried towards him, holding out a small pencil torch. He had been hoping for something more spectacular. 'Does it work?' he asked suspiciously.

Lucy switched it on. The thin beam was wonderfully strong. Lucy blew out the candles and they pressed on towards the water and the gas.

The sound of splashing water had got louder and louder as they had neared the café corridor at the top of the spiralling steps. The first door led to the toilets. Inside there was surprisingly little sign of damage, although a high pipe had fractured and was providing a passable shower.

Alan and Lucy splashed handfuls of the icy cold water into gritty eyes, dry mouths and dust-caked faces. Lucy pushed her whole head into the shower and yelled at the shock and exhilaration. Alan stepped beneath the cascade and lifted his face. They knew they were somehow washing away the fear and pessimism of the last half-hour. Shivering but cleansed, Alan moved off to explore the café and kitchens for food and drink. He suddenly felt hungry.

Lucy heard Alan shove his way through the door and leaned her head into the stream of water, slowly turning to wash as much dust, rubble, dirt, sand and grit from her hair as she could. The coldness was beginning to numb her scalp but – like Alan – she found it bracing. Then the water flow lessened briefly becoming little more than a trickle. Finally it stopped. The sudden silence was unnerving. Lucy blinked to clear her eyes and turned, puzzled, to look where the jagged pipe broke into the cubicle through a section of collapsed wall. The candlelight threw swaying shadows around the lavatory cubicle. She blinked rapidly – then her gaze fastened and the pupils of her eyes widened as her trembling mouth opened and she screamed.

TWELVE

The kitchen was swarming with rats. Caught in the thin, bright beam of Alan's torch they briefly froze before running for cover. He instinctively jammed a fist into his mouth as he saw them pour from the open, overturned freezer like a deadly sleek torrent. Alan took three quick steps backwards and slammed the kitchen door, hoping to shut them in. He began to tremble. It was then that he realised the sound of running water had gone and a strange high-pitched sobbing noise had taken its place.

'Lucy!' he shouted and rushed to the cubicle.

Two rats bobbed and ducked in the hole where the shattered pipe poked through, their bright beady eyes reflected in the flickering candlelight. Alan barged the door open but could not at first see his sister. He yelled and waved his arms at the rats which turned and disappeared instantly. 'Lucy?' he called.

Lucy had retreated behind the door and into the corner. Her eyes were fixed on the dark crevice between the shattered tiles where the rats had appeared. She could not pull her glance away but her whimpering stopped and she slowly sank into a kneeling position. Alan crouched in front of her.

'It's all right,' he whispered. 'They've gone.'

His sister nodded but still could not drag her attention away and her face was so full of fright that Alan turned to make sure the intruders had actually vanished.

'They've gone,' he insisted, standing and trying to draw her from the dirty wet floor. 'Come on, Lucy. You're safe.' He reached up to where the carrier bag hung from a coat peg and found another candle which he lit, and then another. As the light strengthened and the scary shadows disappeared, the terror of the cubicle lessened.

He switched off the torch and turned his attention back to his sister. 'Can you move?'

She nodded and reached for his hand, her eyes still glued to the space between the cracked tiles behind the cistern. Carefully he drew her up and stood directly before her so that her line of vision ended at his own familiar face. Alan saw her eyes soften and refocus on his and he smiled gently. After a while, Lucy opened her mouth, trying to explain but no words came.

'I know,' murmured Alan softly. He shuddered. 'Come on,' he whispered. They slowly left the cubicle and he blew out one of the candles handing the other to Lucy. She took a step towards the kitchen but Alan put an arm round her shoulders and turned her away.

'Can't we get out through the kitchen?' Lucy asked, able to speak at last.

Alan led her firmly away. 'The door's blocked,' he said brusquely. 'I've tried it.'

Lucy saw the eyes of her brother swing briefly away from her and guessed she was being lied to. 'What about the café?'

Alan was uneasy: what if the rats were in there too? He shrugged uncertainly. Lucy took a deep breath and stepped forward to turn the handle on the café door. It would not move. She tried it again then glanced at Alan. 'Do they lock it at night?'

Alan did not know and tried the door himself. It would not shift a centimetre. The icy thrill of the water had gone. They were suddenly two fearful, pale, shivering children who knew their time was running out. They walked silently on, feeling they were getting nowhere.

Cathy's phone began to ring continually as reporters found her number and the inspector set a police guard on the archdeacon's house when a film crew discovered where she was and somehow managed to get into the close.

Mrs Robinson, the organist's wife, fretted in the choir school's common room with other inhabitants of the close, waiting for permission to return to their homes. This is ridiculous, she thought. The cloisters are in no danger. She was glad her husband was staying overnight in Hereford where he had given an organ recital the night before. He would be even more irritated than she was. The cat would expect food.

*

The chief fire officer reported that his team had found a household candle and matches in the wreckage of the Shrine Chapel which supported Cathy Graham's hunch that her children might have gone down there to light a candle. The chief looked round the tense committee. 'And one of the dogs found blood in the treasury. Very little of it,' he added quickly. 'We don't know how they got from the Shrine Chapel up into the treasury but it means they're not badly injured – and that they're thinking.'

Back in her own house, Sara sat by the phone. She hadn't wanted to leave Cathy but she needed to be home when Michael phoned. She knew he would phone as soon as he heard about the cathedral. While she waited, she laid out a quick tarot spread and turned over the two central cards. The first was 'The Knave of Batons' – the card she always associated with Michael – and the second was 'The Sun', which featured twins, a boy and girl. Could Michael actually be in the cathedral, with the Graham kids? She threw a worried glance at the clock.

THIRTEEN

Alan and Lucy wriggled through the narrow crack and torchlight revealed they were in the office and hideaway of Dr Robinson, the cathedral organist. It seemed to have escaped damage – except for the fallen corner which had let them in – but the door out into the nave was firmly fastened from the other side.

Lucy opened a large cupboard fixed to one of the panelling walls. The lower shelves were crammed with anthems and hymn books but on the top shelf stood a bottle of whisky, a glass and a full bottle of mineral water. Best of all, on the shelf below, a large tin of biscuits waited. They pounced.

Alan crammed a final biscuit into his mouth and swilled it down with the last of the clean, safe water. He tipped the rest of the biscuits into the carrier bag as Lucy carefully tested the narrow staircase that led up from the organist's room into the high hollow stone screen on which Archenford Cathedral's famous organ perched.

'It's rickety,' she reported, 'but it's our only way out.'

Alan and Lucy cautiously made their way up

the steep wooden steps. It was a part of the cathedral where neither had ever set foot. Fifteen steps took them to a door, narrow, low and angular. Lucy turned the knob and eased the door open.

They knew instantly where they were. They were inside the massive stone screen – twenty-seven metres high and nearly three metres thick – and halfway up the steps that led from the base of the screen up to the organ.

The moment they stepped from the doctor's private staircase they were back in the dangerous world of the uncertain. The most worrying aspect of all was that, in spite of its huge solidity, the screen had moved. It was obviously tilted several degrees and the walls themselves were scarred and cracked with the tension.

'My God!' murmured Alan. 'If the screen's leaning like this, what's the rest of the cathedral going to be like?' Lucy didn't reply.

Alan shone the torch down the staircase, towards the foot of the screen, but it appeared to be blocked. They could hear unusual sounds too – though Alan recognised them, recalling the eerie singing of the stones as he lay in the pitch black of the Shrine Chapel, stunned and terrified. It meant that, somewhere near them, stone was under pressure, ready to splinter and crack. At least he had Lucy now. They knew where they were and were working their way out.

Alan trudged doggedly up the disturbing angle of steps, trying to balance against the slope and letting his mind run back over the previous hours. Half lost in his thoughts he swung round a corner – then screamed as something tore at his hair, dragging him backwards. He fell heavily down several steps and stared wildly up.

'Sorry.' Lucy looked down at him, breathing heavily. 'Sorry,' she repeated, moving down to kneel at his side.

Alan rubbed his head. 'What's wrong with you? That hurt.' He clambered upright, angrily rubbing his head.

'Not as much as if I'd let you go on,' she said quietly. Alan saw the shock in her face. He slung the carrier bag over his shoulder, picked up the torch and climbed back to where he had been. He tentatively examined the steps as they led round the corner.

His heart jumped. They didn't lead anywhere. There was a sheer drop into darkness.

They couldn't go up and, if they retraced their steps, they would end up either at the blocked staircase or in the dead end of Dr Robinson's room. Alan took a couple of steps back from the abyss and sank down on his haunches, too tired to think what they should do next. He felt Lucy slide alongside and knew she felt the same. Shock and disappointment were wearing them down and, when at last she spoke, her voice was flat and dull. Every muscle felt leaden and aching. 'I think I need to sleep.'

Alan nodded slowly and draped an arm round her shoulders. 'Sorry I shouted at you,' he said gently. She leaned into him and shut her sore eyes.

They were giving up and they knew it. The two children wanted no more responsibility for solving their own situation; they would have to leave it for others. As Lucy dozed Alan tried to turn his thoughts to what might be happening outside.

As they sat there, the stone sang and groaned. Twice Alan heard a distant crash and its hollow echo as some unknown part of the building fell and once there was a sudden scattering of sand as massive stones shifted inside the screen and jerked Lucy awake briefly.

The worst part of it was that his mother might still think them safe at the Vaughans' farm on the Broomyard Downs. He knew she would not want to worry her children with news of the disaster until the familiar security of daylight.

Daylight. On the feast day of Rycharde. Some celebration, he thought. When would daylight come? At about quarter-past seven? And what was the time now? About four? Neither he nor Lucy wore a watch. What would the rescue services be doing? Why hadn't they heard or seen anything of them? Perhaps the building was not yet safe to enter and search. What had caused the collapse of a building which had stood for hundreds of years? Lucy had talked about something fiery but Alan thought it more likely that a bomb must have exploded. He wondered who would target a cathedral. Alan wished he could doze, like Lucy, but he felt too cold. After a while he gently moved Lucy's head from his shoulder and stiffly stood, rubbing his chilled arms and jogging quietly on the spot. He was regretting the icy shower in the café lavatory. Alan moved cautiously up to the edge of the steps and drew the torch from his pocket.

It looked as if the steps that continued upwards to the organ loft had simply fallen in as the huge structure must have juddered and rocked but there was no sign of them. Alan imagined the pile jumbled far below. He was fed up with not being able to see anything clearly – only as flickering possibilities at the edge of the range of tiny candles or the beam of a small torch. And the torch batteries were getting weaker. He switched off the thin beam. He stood still in the darkness. What was that faint smell? It reminded him of RAF Meeston. The pungent smell of hot oil.

Lucy snorted in her fitful sleep as her brother carefully passed by on his way down. He ignored the strange door to Dr Robinson's staircase and descended further, down to the fall of stone and rubble that blocked the way down to the base of the screen.

His first search for a way through was unsuccessful, though he was sure he could feel a slight movement of air across his face. It was strange air; sometimes it seemed warm. Alan shivered and remembered that in his cold state even the smallest rise in air temperature would be noticeable. He switched off the light so that he could concentrate his senses better. He turned his face this way and that, like radar, in an attempt to pinpoint where the hint of hot oil was finding a way through the barrier of fallen stone.

He moved as far to his right as he could. Yes, it was stronger in that one place, close to the wall. He took a step nearer and sniffed again. This time he not only scented oil but felt brief warmth on his cheeks. Alan had the uncanny sense of light that was not from candle or torch. Pink light? It flared again – and then it had gone.

Alan climbed a boulder of granite and twisted between two blocks of shattered masonry, desperate to use that faint impression of light before its whereabouts faded from his mind. He squeezed round a broad pillar and dug out enough rubble to burrow further. He painfully scraped between shattered wooden panelling and a section of rough wall. Alan gasped for breath. He was in a small, confined space and suddenly he flinched, not prepared for the shock of the pink glow that suddenly flared, brighter this time. Redness etched itself on his eyes long after the flare died and Alan blinked several times. The light was coming from an uneven gap at shoulder-height. He slowly approached, still blinking hard to clear the rosy haze, and looked out over the wrecked altar and choirstalls of Archenford Cathedral. At first he refused to believe his eyes.

From outside, strong floodlighting angled up through the long lancet windows dappling the area in patchy blue-white light. Fifty metres away from Alan, heavily impacted among wood and stone, was the unmistakable shape of a burned-out Jaguar, wedged between the roof and the top of the screen. One crumpled wing was just recognisable in the blackened skeleton of twisted metal but there was no sign of the other. Occasional pink flares glowed around the wreck as the last of the oil burned. Alan could just make out a blackened and peeling design. *Lightning*. His father's favourite Jaguar. Alan screamed.

He heard Lucy's anxious shout almost immediately and screamed again, too shocked for words, his mind so reeling that he felt the wreck would disappear if he were to shut off concentration for a second. Then Lucy was at his side, wide-eyed and, like her twin, unable to believe the evidence of her eyes. At last the spell broke.

'Can you see the canopy?' she shouted. If it was not in place, their father would have ejected – but if it was . . . Lucy stared at Alan, her face desperate with the impossible question: how could this have happened? Alan shook his head wildly and they swung back to the gap in the screen.

'Can you see Dad?' Alan cried. They peered into the patchy gloom, screwing up their eyes. At last Lucy forced her attention from *Lightning* and looked down to ground level. The tower door had been torn from its hinges.

'The tower door in the corner's open,' she gasped. 'If we can get up to the first gallery from there, we can reach Dad's plane.' She was already turning from the gap.

'But how do we get down to the choirstalls?' Alan asked.

'Robinson's room,' she called back.

Lucy and Alan swept out the music, hymn

books and photographs and began dragging out the shelves. Lucy's memory had served her well: the cupboard was definitely fixed against the wooden panelling. Alan kicked at it and it gave a hopeful splintering sound. Ten kicks later, exhausted, he made way in the restricted space for Lucy to continue. The stark image of the crumpled Jaguar under the roof drove them on. It took six minutes of frantic kicking before they were able to squeeze through the shattered panelling and stand in the open space near the choirstalls.

It was weird to find themselves out of claustrophobic darkness and in wide space. For once, they did not need torch or candles and they could at last hear the grinding of emergency generators in the close, though there was no time for thoughts of their own rescue. They ran across the open space to the tower door, glancing up at the stone screen looming over them at a crazy angle.

A constable brought Toby Whitmarsh the latest news and the architect traced the twins' imagined course on his plans. He could see the obvious connection between the treasury and the corridor above – the lift shaft – but the shaft was firmly blocked by the largest of the bells and there was no sign of the Graham children below it.

'Perhaps they were already safely on the shop level when the bell fell,' suggested the wing commander.

'I hope so,' muttered Toby. 'But if they

weren't . . .' A call came through on the radio: the search team was about to enter the cathedral shop.

With the floodlit ruins behind him, the chief fire officer read his statement to six microphones in front of four cameras and surrounded by newsmen. It was four o'clock and he tried to keep his mind alert. 'There have been developments since the last statement. We now have good reason to believe that there were people inside the cathedral at the time of the collision. A search team is making its way through the cathedral in an attempt to find them. It is also making reports on the conditions it is meeting and we intend to commit more personnel as soon as possible. I'll take a few questions.'

'Any information on the plane or its pilot?'

'Not yet.'

'How are conditions inside?'

'Highly dangerous.'

'Is it true the people inside are children and that their father is the pilot of the plane?'

The chief's bleeper sounded and he turned away at once. 'That's all. Thank you, gentlemen.'

He opened the door of the caravan. 'What is it?'

No one looked at him. The police inspector spoke quietly. 'A body. In the shop. A boy.' There was a brief silence.

'Get the dean. Get Mrs Graham's doctor. Get that friend of her's – Sara Penn. I want them here at once.' A messenger left and the chief slid back into his seat. Toby Whitmarsh handed him a plastic cup of coffee.

'So the poor girl's on her own,' the wing commander said.

'So long as she doesn't go anywhere near that screen,' said Toby. 'My guess is that it could come down any moment.'

Alan and Lucy ran across the open area. The immaculate Victorian floor tiles were shattered and whole sections of the floor had been forced up. Several of the biggest organ pipes had fallen: one lay with an end propped on the altar and another had speared the bishop's throne and stuck out like a gun barrel. The medieval choir-stalls were wrecked: burning oil had flared through the air and destroyed wherever it had clung. The stench was strong and acrid. They coughed and protected their mouths as they hurried to the open doorway in the foot of the tower pillar.

After the luxury of space and light they were back in the unknown, climbing narrow steps, circling steeply up inside the corner pillar. They were afraid of what they might find but determined to reach the Jaguar as soon as they could. The massive strength of the pillar had kept the staircase intact and they took a brief rest every fifty steps. As they hurried higher they were glad to see a dim light. 'That means the top door's open,' gasped Lucy.

The top door was not open. Like the doorway it once fitted, it no longer existed. Lucy and Alan carefully clambered through the wrecked arch. They were high above floor level and felt giddy and insecure. Now they had to cross the gap where the screen had been torn from the wall. It was no more than a metre across but seemed much much more as they looked anxiously down the sheer drop to the choirstalls. Alan shivered and turned away but Lucy scraped the soles of her trainers on the floor for maximum friction, took two paces back and, trying not to think, jumped across. Alan checked his soles too and, heart in mouth, followed. The next moment he was at her side, trembling, but there was no time to recover. They threaded a path through the mess of rubble, clambered through a chaos of organ pipes and squeezed past the toppled console of the organ.

The airplane was fifteen metres away but the heat made it impossible to go closer. They gingerly stepped round pungent pools of smouldering oil, eyes stinging in the acrid haze. They tried to push nearer, hands over coughing mouths, peering through hot, running eyes at the ruin of the Jaguar.

Webbed and cracked with the heat, darkened by smoke, the canopy was firmly and disastrously in place. Inside, strapped upright, an obscure helmeted figure seemed to be staring straight ahead, concentrating on the blackened wall seven metres away.

Alan gave a low groan and started forward but Lucy held him tight. 'No,' she said softly. 'No, Alan.' He turned anguished eyes on her and briefly struggled but the light in his eyes dulled and his energy deserted. Brother and sister seemed to freeze.

A searchlight wavered over them from the nave below and an excited voice shouted. The thin beam retraced its path and found the motionless pair again. A whistle blew immediately and another beam reached up to enclose them.

The children clung together beneath the cathedral roof, transfixed by the blinding whiteness as a third beam locked on to the wreck of the Jaguar. Far below, a radio crackled and a dog barked. It was answered by another, much closer, but the two silent figures on the screen seemed not to hear. It was as if the beams were holding them up and – if the lights were suddenly turned off – the figures would fold and fall like puppets at the end of a play. The first of the rescue team stepped cautiously on to the screen but Alan and Lucy Graham turned stone faces to him as if he were an intruder on a secret and very private event.

Also available in the HORRORSCOPES series

SAGITTARIUS – MISSING
23 November–21st December

*Employment prospects loom on the horizon but
you are right to be apprehensive. Be careful –
things aren't always what they seem.*

Fifteen-year-old Andrea, usually known as Andi,
gets a job in a crafts shop in the shopping mall.
The proprietor seems a little strange but Andi's
happy enough. She does, however, feel that she's
being watched and finds out that two missing
teenagers had previously worked in the shop.
And then, when she's working late, the lights go
out. Andi panics and runs out of the shop but
too late – the shopping mall's on fire and Andi is
trapped . . .

CAPRICORN – CAPRICORN'S CHILDREN
22nd December–19th January

A relative is behaving strangely but act with caution – this is a dangerous time for you both.

Jan becomes concerned about her brother, Jimmy, who seems to have become withdrawn and quiet. Then she discovers articles in his room published by the Church of Capricorn and, not wanting to confront Jimmy directly, goes to the church herself. The preacher there is a charismatic man but Jan is suspicious about the church's influence over her brother – and then she hears that the congregation plan to kill themselves in a mass suicide. Can she save her brother?

PISCES – REVENGE
19th February–20th March

There is a price to be paid for everything in this life and your payments are now overdue.

While slightly drunk, Danny steals a car and goes joy-riding with his girlfriend, Jo. But there's an accident; Danny hits a girl in the street but, terrified, he drives off. Jo, too drunk at the time to realise what was happening, becomes fascinated by the victim of the accident, Samantha, and goes to visit the now paralysed girl in hospital, concealing her true involvement. But then, as events reach a dramatic climax, Jo discovers too late that Samantha has a thirst for vengeance . . .

ARIES – BLOOD STORM
21st March – 20th April

Loved ones will be making many demands on you. Try to stay calm.

Jack Carter, an architect, is living with his second wife, daughter and two children from his previous marriage. His first wife and son, however, live near by and there are, inevitably, meetings between them. And then strange things begin to happen; Jon's room is trashed, the brakes on Kate's bike fail, Maggie is attacked and later loses control of the car she's driving. The situation is fraught – but what's happening and could it be something to do with someone in the family itself?

TAURUS – MIRROR IMAGE
21st April–20th May

A new friendship will bring delights but also troubles – tread carefully. Someone looks to you to give them strength, but you will need to be brave.

Fifth-former Dianne soon makes friends with the new girl, Jeannette. But soon Dianne and her other friends find that Jeannette has strange mood changes, not to mention the unpleasant things that sometimes happen around her – a boy's hand is trapped in a locker, Dianne's dog is killed and Dianne's baby brother is found with a jar of angry wasps. The friendship continues until an afternoon's boating trip turns into a near-disaster and Dianne begins to feel that there is something quite evil about Jeannette . . .

GEMINI – SLICED APART
21st May–20th June

Avoid confrontations with relatives – there could be unpleasant and unexpected consequences.

Nina has never forgiven her twin, Gemma, for being born first, believing (wrongly) that Gemma is her parents' favourite. Then Nina finds that the boy she has idolised, Daniel, has started going out with Gemma. Overcome with jealousy, Nina begins to think of ways to get rid of her sister – and forges a terrible friendship with a murderer. Will Gemma be safe?

CANCER – BLACK DEATH
21st June–20th July

The sun in Saturn suggests an ominous turn of events. The distant past may come back to haunt you and you should act with caution. A good turn may have unexpected and unpleasant consequences.

A family trip to Maris Caulfield, a village which was wiped out during the plague in the fourteenth century, turns into a nightmare for Janie Hyde. Exploring the village, she discovers a cottage bearing a plaque to the people who lived and died there during the plague years – including a Jayne Hyde. Janie starts to get 'flashbacks', going back in time to watch as Jayne Hyde's life crumbles as those around her die of the plague. But it seems that Jayne's spirit is trying to take over Janie's body and Janie's own life is now in danger . . .

William Sleator

THE SPIRIT HOUSE

Julie Kamen is definitely not looking forward to the arrival of her family's exchange student from Thailand, but Bia is nothing like Julie expects. He turns out to be handsome and sophisticated, and Julie is intrigued by him. She and her brother, Dominic, go out of their way to make Bia feel at home. Dominic even builds a traditional Thai spirit house for Bia, to keep the evil spirits away.

But Bia is afraid of the spirit house, and Julie begins to see why, when the spirit seems to take control of her life as well. Julie is convinced that the spirit is claiming revenge – but for what?

By the author of *The Duplicate*, *Interstellar Pig* and *Strange Attractors*.

'The climax is a shocker . . .'
School Library Journal

Nicholas Pine

TERROR ACADEMY: THE PROM

A girl goes missing down at Thunder Lake after a graduation party gets out of hand. Now, twenty years on at Central Academy, the past is forgotten – or is it?

As Kim Wedman gets the prom committee underway, the fun turns slowly into a terrible nightmare. First it's the mysterious notes, then the murders begin. As she tracks the crimes, the full horror dawns on Kim – has the killer returned from the past?

Nicholas Pine

TERROR ACADEMY: STUDENT BODY

Abby Wilder is a bright and popular senior, a cheerleader and straight-A student. And the victim of an attacker who clearly intended to kill her!

While the police search desperately for clues, Abby's memory of the attack fades completely. But not the strange visions that seem to be warning her: this killer has rampaged before – and is about to strike again . . .

Also available in the Terror Academy *series*

Lights Out
Stalker
Sixteen Candles
Spring Break
The New Kid
Night School
Science Project
Night School
Summer School
The Prom
The In Crowd